Managers, financiers and other Excel users:

- Do your data tables contain **too much information**?

- Can you see **patterns and trends** at a glance?

- Can you figure out the **meaning** of the data?

- Would you like your report to **look like this**:

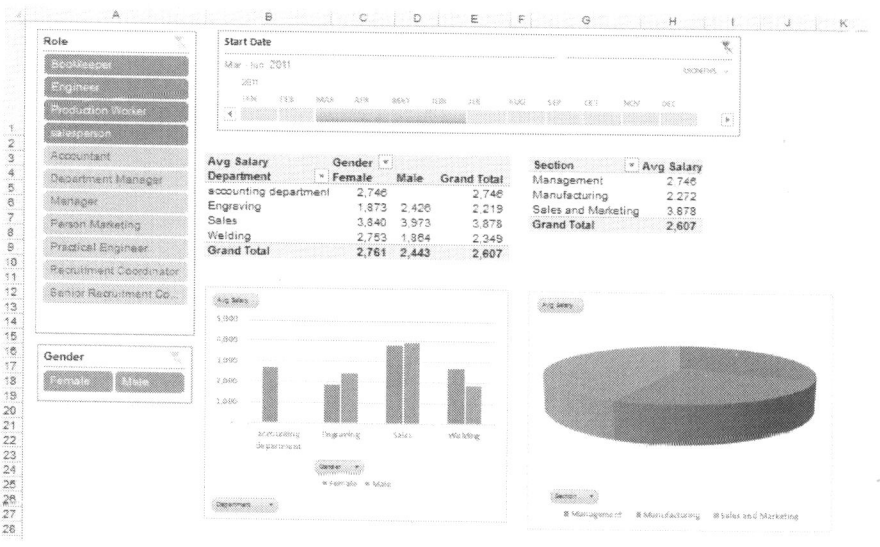

It takes less than 10 minutes!

A pivot table is a simple, yet powerful technique, that enables Excel's users to transform data overload into meaningful and organized knowledge.

With pivot tables you can:

- See the data in dozens of different ways with a simple mouse drag
- Perform fast calculations with no need for formulas
- Focus on another part of the data each time and get a clear picture
- Show more trends and patterns
- Create dozens of reports and charts to analyze your data

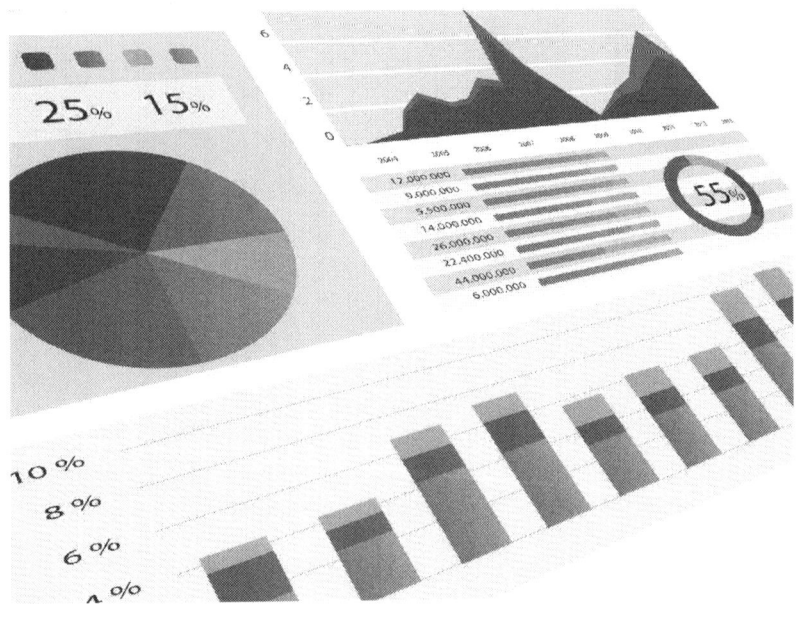

Table of Contents

Introduction 7
Disclaimer 8
What is a Pivot Table? 9
Basic Concepts 13
Conditions to Create a Pivot Table 15
   Necessary conditions 15
   Desirable conditions 16
   Limitations of a pivot table 16
Creating a Pivot Table 19
   Creating the table 19
   Source of Data 20
      Selecting from a data table in the current file 21
      Selecting from a data table in another Excel file 21
   Data Location 22
   Structure of the pivot table 22
      List of fields 24
      Areas 24
   Filters 31
      Multivalued Report Filter 32
   Changing the data source 33
      Creating a pivot table based on a dynamic data table 34
   Refreshing the pivot table 35
      Refreshing a single pivot table 36
      Refreshing all the pivot tables in a file 36
   Exercises 37
Performing Calculations 41
   Changing Calculations 41
   Data display options 43

Percentage of a column total 44

Percentage of a row total 44

Percentage of a grand total 47

Running total 48

Percentage of 52

Data Grouping 54

Grouping numeric data 55

Date Grouping 58

Grouping textual data 61

Multivalued Report 63

Calculated Field 65

Calculation based on a single field 65

Calculation based on several fields in a pivot table 67

Deleting a calculated field 71

Calculated Item 72

Exercises 78

Changing the Report Structure 81

Switching columns and rows 81

Adding columns or rows 83

Adding a page break between items 85

Exercises 88

Formatting Pivot Tables 89

Structure Format 89

Subtotals 89

Sorting 91

Filtering 93

Slicers 98

Creating filters using slicers: 99

Manipulating Slicers 102

Removing items which were deleted from the data source ... 104

The Timeline 105
    Insert Timeline: 105
    Changing the time period: 107
    Changing the Timeline's appearance: 107
Exercises 109

Design Tab 111
Layout category 111
Pivot table style options 112
Quick design styles of pivot table 112
    Choosing a new style 112
Exercises 114

Charts 115
Adding a chart to an existing pivot table 115
Simultaneously creating a pivot table and a chart 117
Exercises 118

Tips and Tricks 119
Using Recommended PivotTables 119
Quickly creating a pivot table 120
Obtaining the data source 120
Creating Tabs from Filters 121
Filter Locations 124
GetPivotData 126
Sorting the field list 127
Repeating the item labels 129

Advanced Uses of Pivot Tables 131
Finding unique records and duplicate records 131
Human Resources Planning 134
Cash Flow 136
Profit and Loss 138

Appendix 141
Selecting data from other file types 141

5

Pivot Tables Wizard 144

Multiple Consolidation Ranges 147

The Data Model **153**

Basic terms in databases 154

Relationships 154

Types of Relationship 156

Primary key 159

Foreign key 159

Creating a pivot table based on two or more tables 162

Creating the pivot table 162

Creating Relationships 165

Forming a relationship (One to Many): 165

Forming a relationship (One to One): 166

Creating the Relationship 167

Dragging the fields 169

Distinct Count Functions 171

The data model limitations 175

Grouping 175

Calculated fields and calculated items 175

Refresh 176

Displaying the data source (Drill Down) 176

Epilogue **177**

*_Introduction_*

This book teaches experienced Excel users how to use pivot tables, one of Microsoft Excel's most powerful tools, for quick and efficient data analysis and to minimize formulae usage.

This book was written for Excel 2013 users. However, since the differences between Excel 2013 and Excel 2010 or Excel 2007 are negligible and mainly manifested by the different groups or tabs in the ribbon, users of the older versions can use this book as well.

We would like to thank all of those who took the time to read the book's draft, examining its readability and therefore ensuring that it offers new possibilities to Excel users.

The main difference between pivot tables in Excel 2013 and the older versions concerns the "Data Model" which will be dealt with in the appendix.

Disclaimer

This book was written specifically for Microsoft Excel users who seek to extend and enhance their ability to analyze data from various sources.

Many efforts were made to write a complete and reliable book about pivot tables. However, the authors are not responsible for any consequences, loss or damage to any individual or organization which may result by using the information provided in this book.

We recommend backing up your data before any changes are carried out using this book.

What is a Pivot Table?

Databases contain raw data on various topics, and are usually arranged in a tabular form. In many cases, data overload may make it difficult to use the information and convert it into relevant knowledge.

A pivot table is a simple, yet powerful, technique which enables Excel users to turn the data overload into well-organized and meaningful knowledge.

By using a pivot table, users can perform various calculations on their data, such as calculating the average, counting, finding the minimum and the maximum values and so on.

Furthermore, the pivot table enables us to filter and sort the data easily and quickly.

Users may focus on some or all parts of the data, even when the data tables are huge (some databases may contain a million or more records); thus users can obtain their desired data clearly and concisely.

A single data table can be used to create dozens of reports and charts for analyzing the data, with many cross-sections, simply by dragging fields to the appropriate locations.

Thus, the pivot table enables us to better understand processes and trends. It is also a useful tool for decision making.

The pivot table data can be based on an existing Excel file or on other databases (i.e. Access or an SQL-based database).

Since a picture is worth a thousand words, here are some examples of pivot tables, derived from the same database, which show the details of factory employees:

Employee No.	Start Date	Section	Department	Role	Gender	City	Monthly Salary
W1331	02/01/2005	Sales and Marketing	Marketing	Person Marketing	Female	Detroit	2,875
W1332	09/09/2005	Sales and Marketing	Marketing	Person Marketing	Female	Detroit	3,031
W1333	09/02/2009	Sales and Marketing	Marketing	Person Marketing	Female	Los Angeles	3,035
W1334	06/07/2007	Sales and Marketing	Marketing	Person Marketing	Female	Detroit	3,293
W1335	12/11/2009	Sales and Marketing	Marketing	Person Marketing	Female	Detroit	3,253
W1336	06/05/2005	Sales and Marketing	Marketing	Person Marketing	Female	Los Angeles	3,136
W1337	02/05/2002	Sales and Marketing	Marketing	Person Marketing	Female	Detroit	3,346
W1338	01/03/2003	Sales and Marketing	Marketing	Person Marketing	Male	Miami	2,864
W1339	03/10/2006	Sales and Marketing	Marketing	Person Marketing	Male	San Diego	3,178
W1340	04/11/2005	Sales and Marketing	Marketing	Person Marketing	Female	Detroit	3,007
W1341	11/05/2006	Sales and Marketing	Marketing	Person Marketing	Female	Los Angeles	3,027
W1112	02/12/2003	Sales and Marketing	Sales	salesperson	Male	New Jersey	3,741
W1113	04/09/2011	Sales and Marketing	Sales	salesperson	Male	Miami	4,015
W1114	06/08/2005	Sales and Marketing	Sales	salesperson	Female	Los Angeles	4,189
W1115	05/07/2008	Sales and Marketing	Sales	salesperson	Male	San Diego	3,651
W1116	04/06/2009	Sales and Marketing	Sales	salesperson	Male	Detroit	3,906
W1117	03/08/2004	Sales and Marketing	Sales	salesperson	Male	New Jersey	3,785
W1118	08/06/2011	Sales and Marketing	Sales	salesperson	Female	Detroit	3,707
W1119	02/05/2004	Sales and Marketing	Sales	salesperson	Female	New Jersey	3,916
W1120	07/12/2007	Sales and Marketing	Sales	salesperson	Female	Los Angeles	4,085
W1121	03/12/2010	Sales and Marketing	Sales	salesperson	Male	New Jersey	4,250
W1122	10/10/2001	Sales and Marketing	Sales	salesperson	Male	San Diego	4,241
W1123	02/01/2011	Sales and Marketing	Sales	salesperson	Male	Miami	3,666
W1124	04/01/2003	Sales and Marketing	Sales	salesperson	Female	Detroit	4,397
W1125	01/05/2011	Sales and Marketing	Sales	salesperson	Male	Los Angeles	3,662
W1126	08/11/2008	Sales and Marketing	Sales	salesperson	Female	Detroit	4,349
W1127	06/04/2008	Sales and Marketing	Sales	salesperson	Male	Miami	3,973
W1128	02/10/2006	Sales and Marketing	Sales	salesperson	Female	Los Angeles	3,661
W1129	12/04/2011	Sales and Marketing	Sales	salesperson	Female	Los Angeles	3,682
W1130	01/12/2002	Sales and Marketing	Sales	salesperson	Female	New Jersey	4,276

The following pivot tables were derived from the database above:

Number of employees in each department:

Department	Count of Employee No.
Accounting	3
accounting department	6
Engraving	453
headquarters	3
Human Resources	9
Marketing	12
Sales	204
Welding	310
Grand Total	1000

Distribution of genders in each department:

Count of Employee No.	Gender	
Department	Female	Male
Accounting	2	1
accounting department	4	2
Engraving	226	227
headquarters	2	1
Human Resources	4	5
Marketing	9	3
Sales	106	98
Welding	144	166

Average salary in each department:

Average of Monthly Salary Department	Total
Accounting	4,551.00
Accounting department	2,947.67
Engraving	2,027.04
Headquarters	4,730.33
Human Resources	3,037.22
Marketing	3,195.75
Sales	3,999.12
Welding	2,127.72
Grand Total	2,504.88

Average salary in each section, by role:

Average of Monthly Salary Role	Management	Manufacturing	Sales and Marketing
Accountant	4,551		
Bookkeeper	2,773		
Department Manager	5,140	4,602	4,449
Engineer		7,474	
Manager	3,864	3,920	4,206
Person Marketing			3,095
Practical Engineer		7,385	
Production Worker		1,827	
Recruitment Coordinator	1,843		
salesperson			3,999
Senior Recruitment Coordinator	4,737		
Grand Total	3,359	2,071	3,957

Basic Concepts

This chapter presents basic concepts relating to pivot tables. While studying and practicing, the following concepts will become clearer:

Subject	Explanation
Data Table	A raw data set, arranged in a table. This can be used as the source of a pivot table.
Pivot Table	A table that displays data in different intersections, as described in this book.
Column	A vertical section of the table consisting of data of the same type, i.e. first name, ID, city etc.
Field	The column's header is called a "field."

Cell	The cell is the intersection of a row and a column, and contains the data of the table.
Item	The data in a cell. For example, New York and Detroit are items in the "City" field.
Record	A data collection which appears in one row and belongs to the same entity, e.g. all the table data which displays information regarding one person: 	Name	St. and No.	City	 |---|---|---| 	John Smith	1 Lexington	New York	

Conditions to Create a Pivot Table

Necessary conditions

- Each column must have a title.

- The title should be written in a single row.

- In a column, all the items should be of the same data type (numbers, dates or strings).

- The data table should not contain any merged cells.

- The data table should not contain subtotals or grand totals.

- Empty rows or columns should not remain within the table (if an empty row or column remains, Excel will treat the table as two different ones).

- After creating a pivot table, do not change the titles of the fields, otherwise the pivot table values will be deleted.

Desirable conditions

- Unique names for each column (when two fields are given the same name, the title of the second field will be appended at end with 2, i.e. "salary2").

- Complete data for all records (when data is missing, the calculations will only be applied to the available records. This can be observed in the cases of calculations such as averages, etc).

Limitations of a pivot table

Subject	Limitation
Number of pivot table reports in the worksheet	Limited by the available memory
Unique items for each field	1,048,576
Row fields or column fields in the pivot table report	Limited by the available memory

Subject	Limitation
Report filter in the pivot table report	256 (May be limited by the available memory)
Value fields in the pivot table report	256
Formulas for calculated items in the pivot table report	Limited by the available memory

Please note:

Due to the limitations of the pivot table, and depending on your personal computer data, you may prefer to save the exercises appearing in this book in a separate file or worksheet for each chapter.

Creating a Pivot Table

Creating a pivot table is a fast procedure, consisting of three simple stages:

1. Selecting the data source and table location.

2. Dragging in the desirable fields.

3. Using the tools in the ribbon for calculations and formatting (most of them can be operated by right-clicking the corresponding area in the pivot table).

Creating the table

1. Place the cursor in a cell within the data table.

2. In the **INSERT** tab, click on the "**PivotTable**" button:

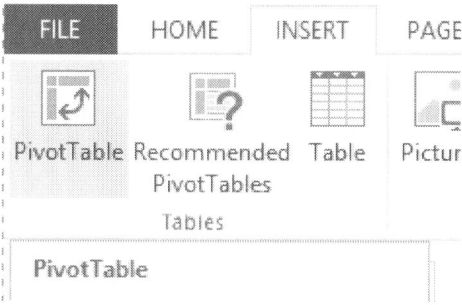

3. The following window will appear:

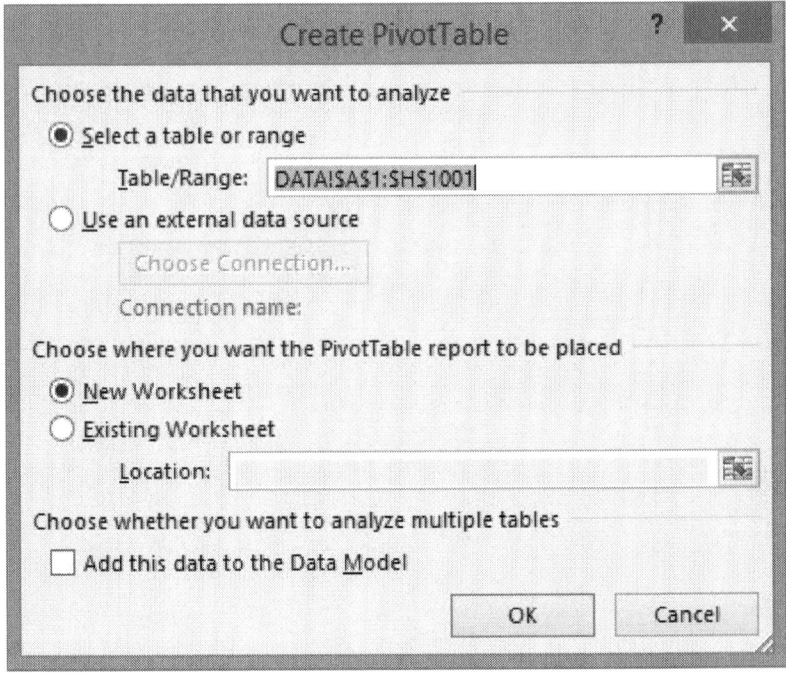

4. In this window, select:

   - The data source to be analyzed (see the "**Source of Data**" section below).

   - The desired location of the pivot table report (see the "**Data Location**" section on page 22).

5. Click [OK]

Source of Data

The data source for the pivot table can be:

- The current Excel file

- Another Excel file

- Other file types, such as:

    o Access

    o SQL database

Selecting from a data table in the current file

1. Once you have pressed **INSERT ⟶ PivotTable** according to the instructions on page 19, the entire table will be selected automatically.

2. The range can be modified by dragging and selecting another range.

Selecting from a data table in another Excel file

1. Before creating a pivot table, make sure that the file that contains the data table is open.

2. Using the Windows task bar, select the data file.

3. Select the desired range.

To read about creating pivot tables from other data types, see page 141.

Data Location

The report can be placed in the same worksheet as the data table, or in another worksheet.

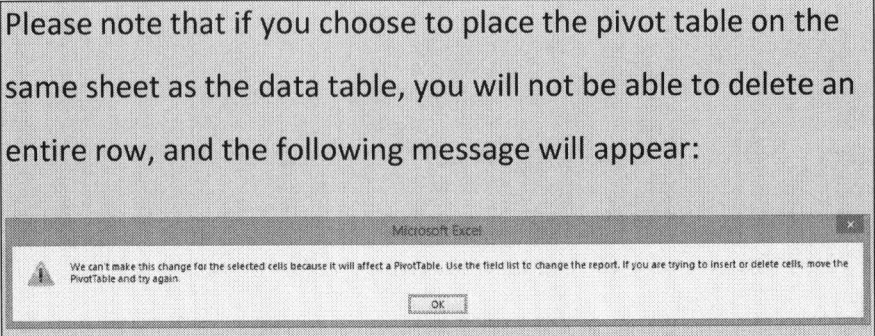

Structure of the pivot table

After selecting the data source and the location, an empty pivot table will appear in the worksheet.

Now you can drag the appropriate fields in, and perform the desired calculations, as shown in the following figure:

The screen is divided into three areas:

- The list of fields

- The pivot table areas

- The pivot table

List of fields

The list of fields contains the column titles of the selected range.

> **Tip:**
> - It is preferable to give the fields short names, since they will appear as titles in the pivot table.
> - Avoid using the words "sum", "average", "minimum", or "maximum" in the titles, since they are added automatically when calculations are performed. This will prevent titles like "Sum of Sum of Salaries" from appearing.

Areas

The pivot table is divided into four areas that the desired fields can be dragged into:

- **COLUMNS** - where fields to be shown in columns are dragged.
- **ROWS** - where fields to be shown in rows are dragged.

- **VALUES** - where fields on which calculations are to be performed (average, minimum, maximum, count, standard deviation, etc.) are dragged.

- **FILTERS** – where fields to be used as a filter are dragged.

The COLUMNS and ROWS form the pivots of the pivot table, as shown in the next figure:

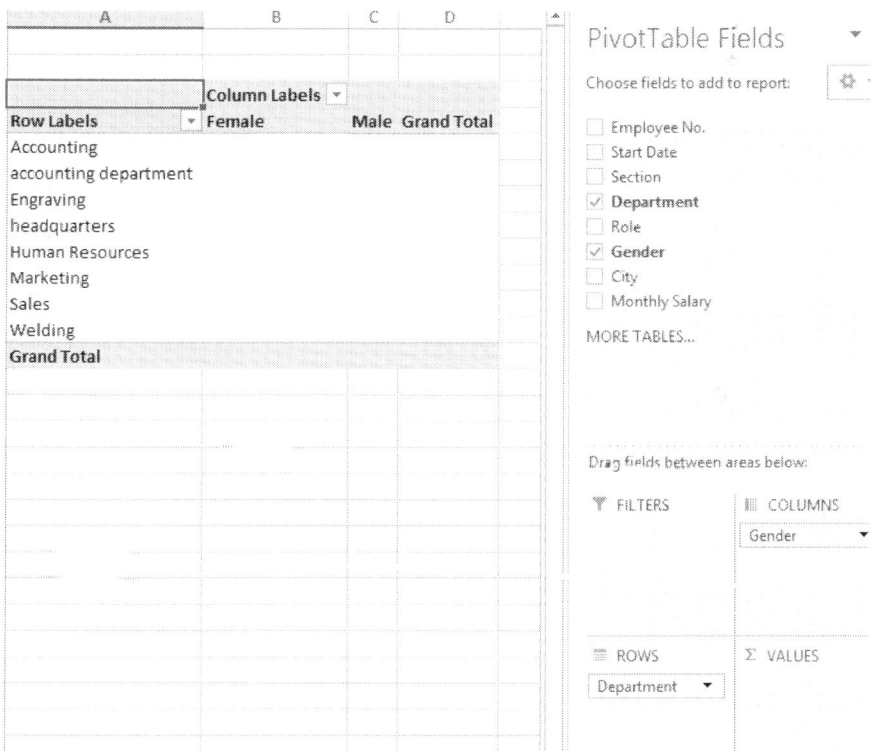

In the figure above, the Department appears in the ROWS, and the Gender appears in the COLUMNS (no calculation is performed at this stage).

Values are data which enable calculations and are dragged into the "VALUES" region, as in the following example:

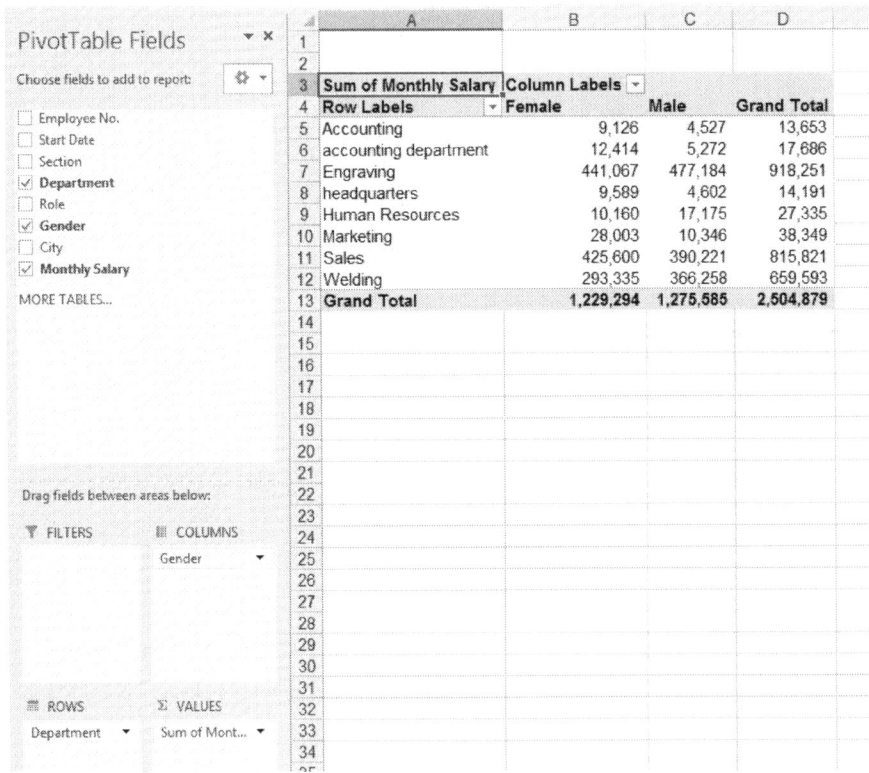

In this example, the "Monthly Salary" field is dragged into VALUES.

The pivot table now displays the salaries paid in each department (the data was formatted with no decimal places and with a thousandths separator).

> Note that by default, Excel summarizes numeric data and counts textual and date data types.

An important note:

Dragging the fields to the ROWS or COLUMNS of the pivot table, creates the title "Row Labels" or "Column Labels", respectively, as shown in the following figure:

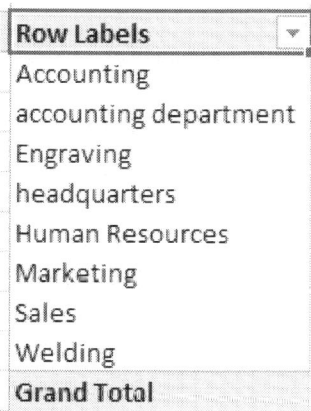

To display the actual field names (and not the title "Row Labels" or "Column Labels"), follow these steps:

1. Click the "**ANALYZE**" Tab.

2. Click "**Options**":

3. In the new window, select the "**Display**" tab:

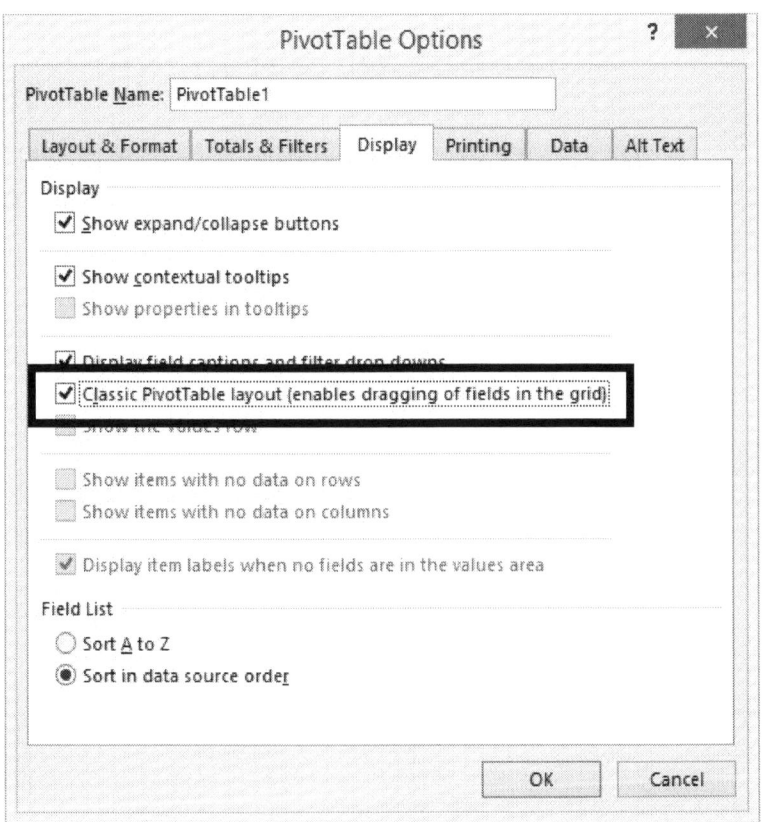

4. Check the "**Classic PivotTable layout**" option.

5. The field name will now appear instead of "row label":

Please note that checking the "**Classic PivotTable Layout**" option enables direct dragging of fields into the pivot table itself, or into the desired area at the bottom of the screen, as shown in the following figure:

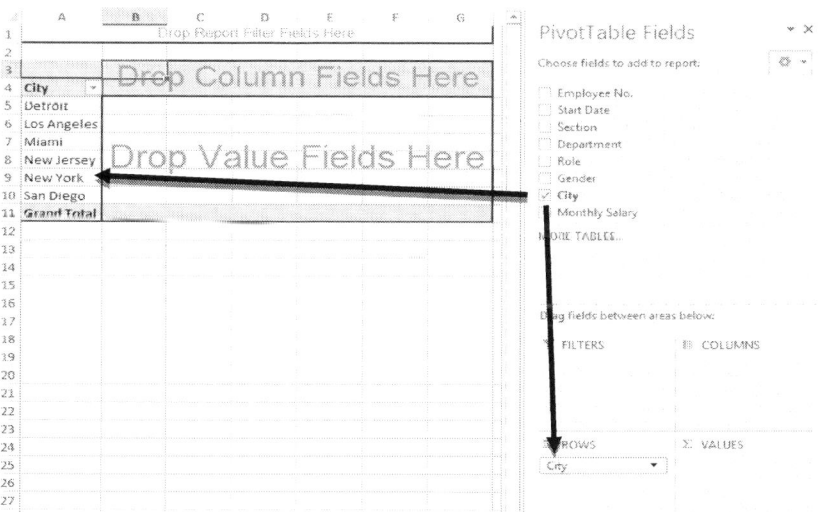

29

In this example, the "City" field is dragged into the ROWS.

The city names listed under the "City" field appear in the pivot table, and each item appears in a different row.

Other fields can be dragged into the ROWS as well (and also into the COLUMNS). In the following example, the "Gender" field was dragged under the field "City."

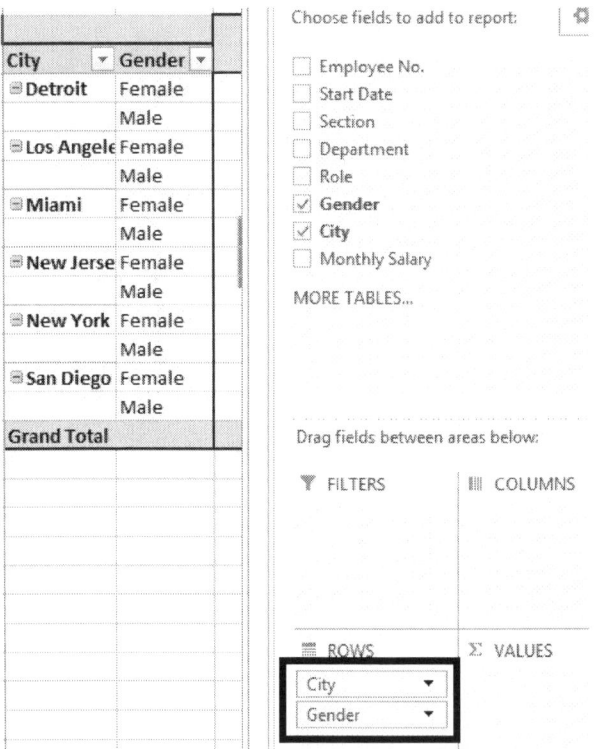

City names listed under the field "City" are shown in the pivot table, and each "City" field is distributed by gender.

Filters

As we have learned before, the fields that form the pivots of the data need to be placed in the ROWS or COLUMNS. Excel also allows us to use those fields as an additional filter for the pivot table.

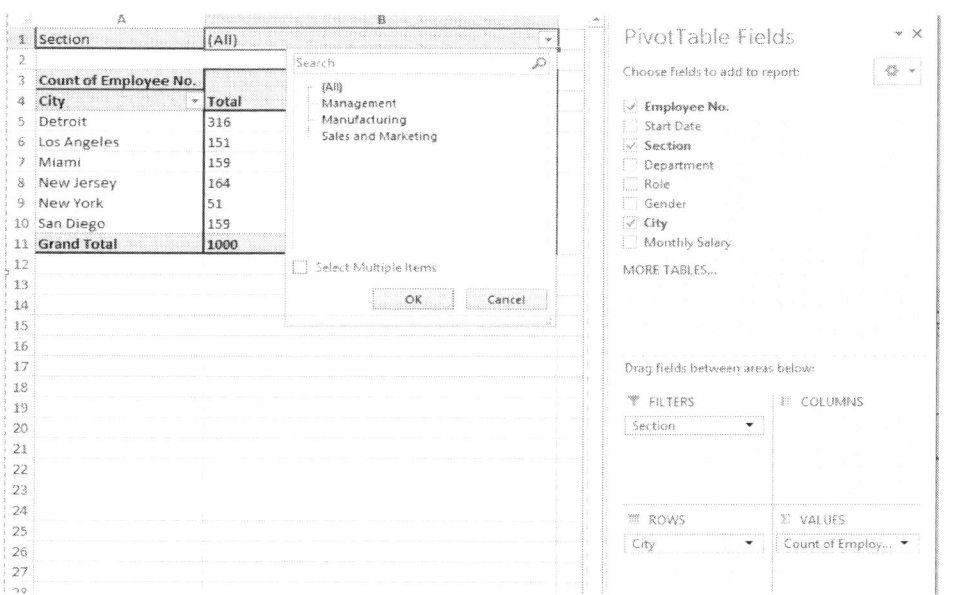

In the example above, the "Section" field was dragged into the FILTERS.

Now we are free to display any of the relevant data in the pivot table:

Section	Management ⊤
Count of Employee No. City	Total
Detroit	6
Los Angeles	2
Miami	6
New Jersey	2
New York	1
San Diego	2
Grand Total	19

In the example above, we sought to show the number of employees in each city and, using the FILTER, we reduced the information to display the management employees only.

Please note that the icon next to the filter changes to ⊤, to indicate that the data displayed in the table is filtered.

Multivalued Report Filter

By default, only one item can be selected using the filter.

To select multiple items, check the "**Select Multiple Items**" box.

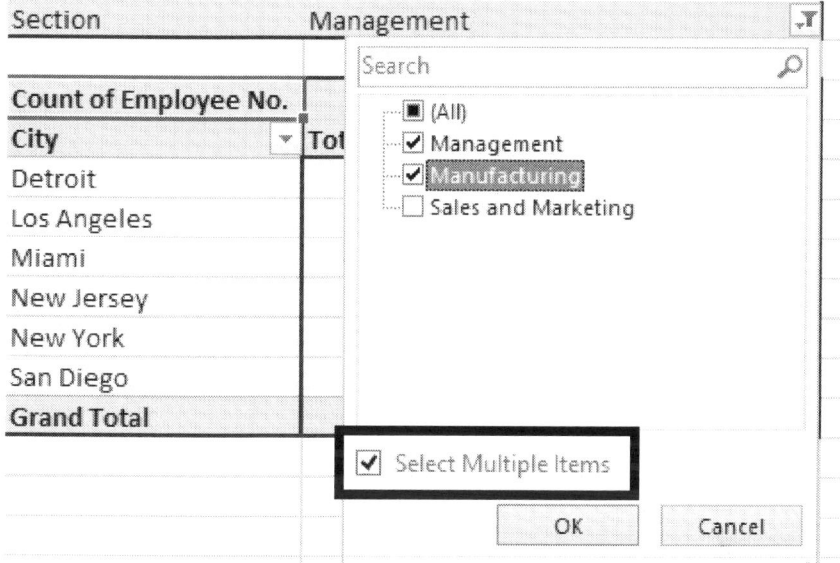

We can now select multiple items to be displayed in the pivot table.

Changing the data source

After creating the pivot table, the original data range may change.

To apply the new range to the pivot table, select "**PIVOTTABLE TOOLS**" tab ⟶ "**ANALYZE**" tab ⟶"**Change Data Source**".

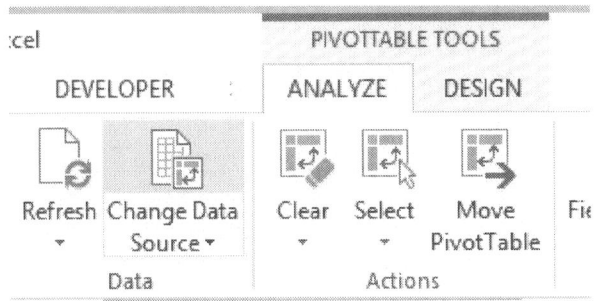

The following window for selecting a new data range will appear:

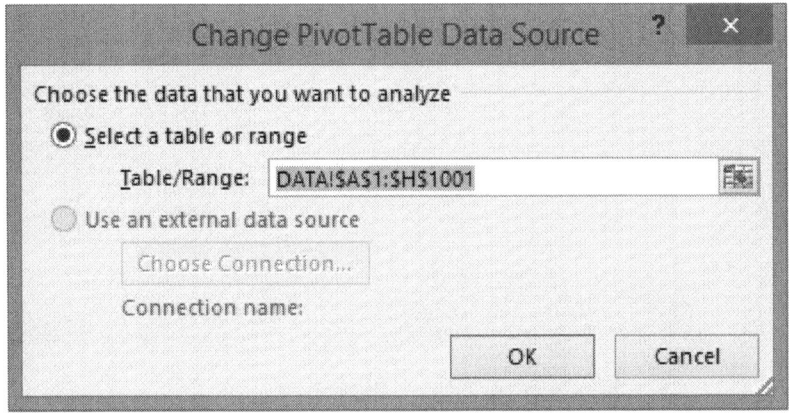

Select the desired range and click OK

Creating a pivot table based on a dynamic data table

If the data range that the pivot table is based on might change in size, It is recommended to base the pivot table on a dynamic table:

1. Place the cursor on the data table.

2. Select "**INSERT**" → "Table".

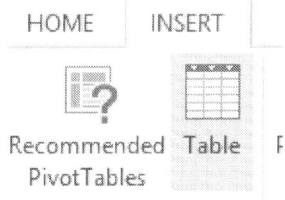

The data table is now changed into a dynamic table:

	A	B	C	D
1	Employee No	Start Date	Section	Department
2	W1000	12/06/2007	Manufacturing	headquarters
3	W1001	11/05/2007	Sales and Marketing	headquarters
4	W1002	05/10/2008	Management	headquarters
5	W1003	08/10/2009	Manufacturing	Welding
6	W1004	03/04/2004	Manufacturing	Engraving
7	W1005	08/12/2001	Sales and Marketing	Sales
8	W1006	09/08/2008	Sales and Marketing	Marketing
9	W1007	12/06/2001	Management	accounting department
10	W1008	11/12/2004	Management	Human Resources

The pivot table based on this dynamic data table will be updated whenever the dynamic table changes in size (you may need to refresh the pivot table).

Refreshing the pivot table

After adding or updating the data table (e.g. changing the data or adding new records), the pivot table based on it has to be refreshed, since it is not updated automatically.

You can refresh a single pivot table or all the pivot tables in the workbook.

Refreshing a single pivot table

1. Place the cursor on the pivot table you want to refresh.
2. Select the "**ANALYZE**" tab from "**PIVOTTABLE TOOLS**" tab.
3. Click "**Refresh**".

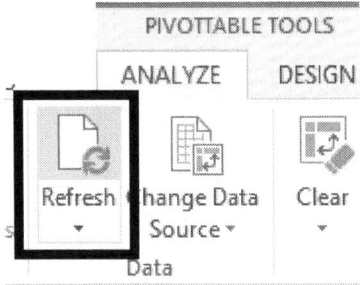

Refreshing all the pivot tables in a file

1. Place the cursor on any pivot table.
2. The "**PIVOTTABLE TOOLS**" tab will appear.
3. Select the "**ANALYZE**" tab.
4. Select the arrow under the "**Refresh**" icon.

5. Select "**Refresh All**".

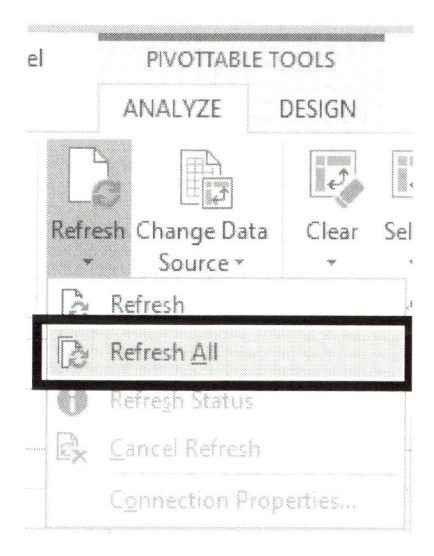

Alternatively, in order to skip the above steps, you may add the "**Refresh All**" icon to the quick access toolbar.

Exercises

For practice, use the "cars.xlsx" file.

You can download it from here:

http://bit.ly/1E3viLd

Please note that you can drag any of the fields to any of the areas. The resulting layouts will display the correct data, but they might be difficult to read and analyze. It is therefore recommended to "play" with the field locations, to figure out which of the layout types is the easiest to understand.

Creating pivot table reports with a column and a row

1. Display the number of cars of each make (the number of cars will be displayed by counting the license numbers).
2. Display the number of cars of each make, by color.
3. Display the number of cars of each make, by color and year of manufacture.
4. Display the number of cars of each make, by color, year of manufacture and gear type.

Creating pivot table reports with a report filter

1. Display the average sales price, by gear type. Add a filter which contains the "Country of Manufacture" field.
2. In the filter created above, display only the cars manufactured in the USA.
3. In the filter created above, display only the cars manufactured in European countries (remember to check the "Select Multiple Items" box).

4. Display the desirable average price by year of manufacture, when "Type of Gear" is used as a report filter.

Refreshing the pivot table data

1. Display a maximum requested sale price by model.
2. Change the price of the first car in the worksheet to 50,000 USD. Has any change occurred in the pivot table? (If not, did you remember to refresh?)

Performing Calculations

Changing Calculations

As we have learned before, a pivot table summarizes numeric data by default, and counts textual data and dates.

However, you may change the type of calculation, according to your needs.

Looking at the example on page 29, we can see that the pivot table summed up the salaries of the employees in each department. Although such a calculation is effective when the desire is to plan the company budget for the next year, we may also want to compare different departments. In order to do that, we need to find the average salary of each department.

To change the calculation type:

- Place the cursor on any cell of the "Monthly Salary" column.
- Right-click and select "Summarize Values By".

- Select the desired calculation type, as shown in the following image:

Row Labels	Sum of Monthly Salary
Accounting	13,653
accounting department	17,686
Engraving	918,251
headquarters	
Human Resources	
Marketing	
Sales	
Welding	
Grand Total	

Context menu options:
- Copy
- Format Cells...
- Number Format...
- Refresh
- Sort ▶
- Remove "Sum of Monthly Salary"
- Summarize Values By ▶
- Show Values As ▶
- Show Details
- Value Field Settings...
- PivotTable Options...
- Hide Field List

Summarize Values By submenu:
- ✓ Sum
- Count
- Average
- Max
- Min
- Product
- More Options...

- The following pivot table will appear:

Department	Average of Monthly Salary
Accounting	4,551.00
Accounting department	2,947.67
Engraving	2,027.04
Headquarters	4,730.33
Human Resources	3,037.22
Marketing	3,195.75
Sales	3,999.12
Welding	2,127.72
Grand Total	**2,504.88**

Please note that the row at the bottom is always labeled as "**Grand Total**", no matter what calculation type is being used for values.

Data display options

In addition to the basic calculations, Excel enables you to display data in advanced forms, such as distribution, running total and more.

To display the data, simply right-click an item in the relevant field of the pivot table itself.

The following window will appear, enabling you to choose between various options:

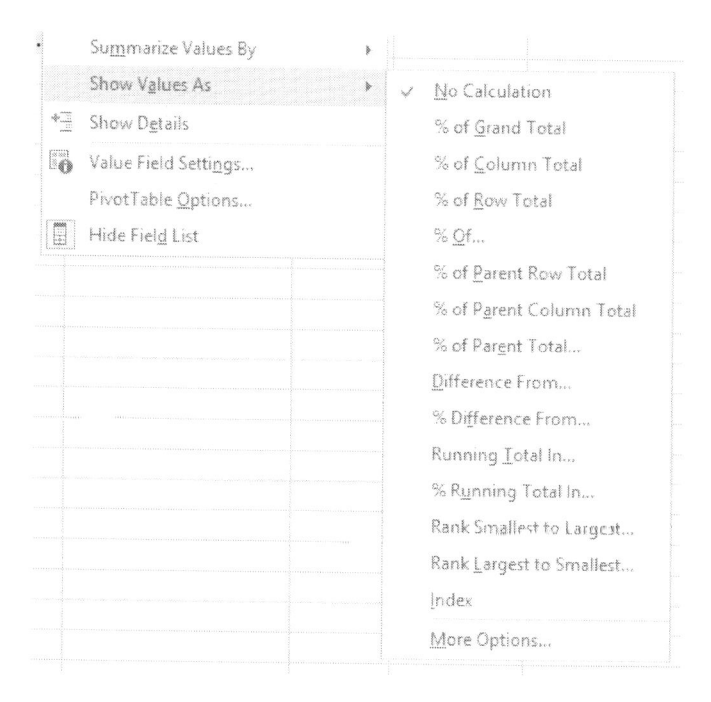

- Summarize Values By
- Show Values As
- Show Details
- Value Field Settings...
- PivotTable Options...
- Hide Field List

- ✓ No Calculation
- % of Grand Total
- % of Column Total
- % of Row Total
- % Of...
- % of Parent Row Total
- % of Parent Column Total
- % of Parent Total...
- Difference From...
- % Difference From...
- Running Total In...
- % Running Total In...
- Rank Smallest to Largest...
- Rank Largest to Smallest...
- Index
- More Options...

Percentage of a column total

This shows the distribution of each item out of the total column:

Department	Sum of Monthly Salary
Accounting	0.55%
accounting department	0.71%
Engraving	36.66%
headquarters	0.57%
Human Resources	1.09%
Marketing	1.53%
Sales	32.57%
Welding	26.33%
Grand Total	100.00%

From here we can learn, for example, that the salary in the Engraving Department constitutes 36.66% of the total salaries of the factory employees, while the salary in the Division Headquarters is only 0.57%.

Percentage of a row total

This displays the distribution of an item out of the entire row.

The following examples illustrate the difference between the percentage of a column total and the percentage of a row total.

We have created a pivot table which displays the number of employees in each role, divided by gender:

Count of Employee No. Role	Gender Female	Male	Grand Total
Accountant	2	1	3
Bookkeeper	3	2	5
Department Manager	2	1	3
Engineer	6	11	17
Manager	1	5	6
Person Marketing	9	2	11
Practical Engineer	4	11	15
Production Worker	360	369	729
Recruitment Coordinator	3	2	5
salesperson	106	97	203
Senior Recruitment Coordinator	1	2	3
Grand Total	497	503	1000

As the table shows, among the employees there are 106 saleswomen and 97 salesmen. It is also evident that the factory employs 9 women and 2 men in marketing.

But what if we need to know what percentage of men in the factory are salesmen? Or what percentage of the women are saleswomen?

We have to display the data as a percentage of a column total:

Count of Employee No.	Gender		
Role	Female	Male	Grand Total
Accountant	0.40%	0.20%	0.30%
Bookkeeper	0.60%	0.40%	0.50%
Department Manager	0.40%	0.20%	0.30%
Engineer	1.21%	2.19%	1.70%
Manager	0.20%	0.99%	0.60%
Person Marketing	1.81%	0.40%	1.10%
Practical Engineer	0.80%	2.19%	1.50%
Production Worker	72.43%	73.36%	72.90%
Recruitment Coordinator	0.60%	0.40%	0.50%
salesperson	**21.33%**	**19.28%**	**20.30%**
Senior Recruitment Coordinator	0.20%	0.40%	0.30%
Grand Total	**100.00%**	**100.00%**	**100.00%**

We can now see that saleswomen constitute 21.33% of the total number of women and salesmen are 19.28% of the total number of men.

We may ask another question: among salespeople, what is the percentage of men and what is the percentage of women?

For this purpose, we present the data as a "percentage of a column total"

Count of Employee No. Role	Gender Female	Male	Grand Total
Accountant	66.67%	33.33%	100.00%
Bookkeeper	60.00%	40.00%	100.00%
Department Manager	66.67%	33.33%	100.00%
Engineer	35.29%	64.71%	100.00%
Manager	16.67%	83.33%	100.00%
Person Marketing	81.82%	18.18%	100.00%
Practical Engineer	26.67%	73.33%	100.00%
Production Worker	49.38%	50.62%	100.00%
Recruitment Coordinator	60.00%	40.00%	100.00%
salesperson	52.22%	47.78%	100.00%
Senior Recruitment Coordinator	33.33%	66.67%	100.00%
Grand Total	49.70%	50.30%	100.00%

We can see that among all salespeople, women constitute 52.22% and men constitute the remaining 47.78%.

Percentage of a grand total

This displays the distribution out of the entire data.

In the following example, we can see the percentages of men and women, divided by role, out of the entire workforce.

Count of Employee No.	Gender		
Role	Female	Male	Grand Total
Accountant	0.20%	0.10%	0.30%
Bookkeeper	0.30%	0.20%	0.50%
Department Manager	0.20%	0.10%	0.30%
Engineer	0.60%	1.10%	1.70%
Manager	0.10%	0.50%	0.60%
Person Marketing	0.90%	0.20%	1.10%
Practical Engineer	0.40%	1.10%	1.50%
Production Worker	36.00%	36.90%	72.90%
Recruitment Coordinator	0.30%	0.20%	0.50%
salesperson	10.60%	9.70%	20.30%
Senior Recruitment Coordinator	0.10%	0.20%	0.30%
Grand Total	49.70%	50.30%	100.00%

We can see, for example, that out of the total number of factory employees, saleswomen constitute 10.60%, while salesmen constitute 9.70%.

Running total

Pivot tables allow us to calculate the running total of the data table.

In the next table, we can see the business cash flow, including revenues and expenses (including future revenues and expenses) on different dates.

Please note that there is no need to sort the table by dates.

Row Labels	Sum of Amount
1/2/2012	453
1/5/2012	407
1/8/2012	-594
1/11/2012	-434
1/14/2012	-2482
1/17/2012	-3661
1/20/2012	-2852
1/23/2012	-2416
1/26/2012	-3044
1/29/2012	731
2/1/2012	-850
2/4/2012	646

Drag the fields to the proper areas, as shown below:

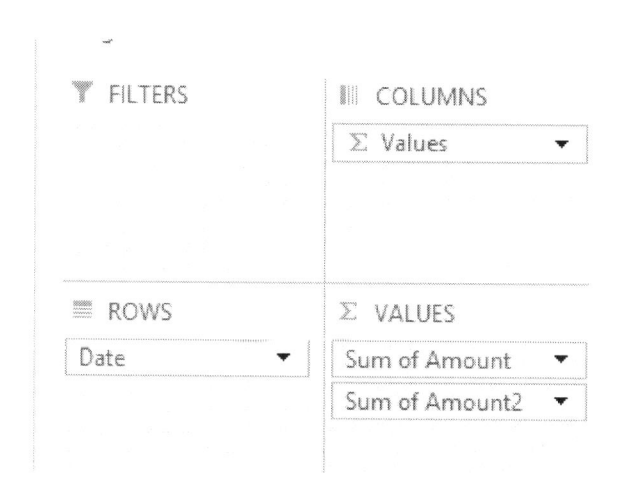

```
▼ FILTERS              ▌▌▌ COLUMNS
                       Σ Values

≡ ROWS                 Σ VALUES
Date          ▼        Sum of Amount    ▼
                       Sum of Amount2   ▼
```

The following pivot table appears:

49

Row Labels	Sum of Amount	Sum of Amount2
1/2/2012	453	453
1/5/2012	407	407
1/8/2012	-594	-594
1/11/2012	-434	-434
1/14/2012	-2482	-2482
1/17/2012	-3661	-3661
1/20/2012	-2852	-2852
1/23/2012	-2416	-2416
1/26/2012	-3044	-3044
1/29/2012	731	731
2/1/2012	-850	-850
2/4/2012	646	646
2/7/2012	14	14
2/10/2012	2353	2353
2/13/2012	3411	3411
2/16/2012	-33	-33
2/19/2012	329	329
2/22/2012	279	279
2/25/2012	611	611
2/28/2012	-3565	-3565
3/2/2012	-2889	-2889

Please note: at this stage, the two sum columns are identical. We now want to turn the second sum column into a running total.

Right-click an item in the second sum column. Select "**Show Values As**", and then select "**Running Total In**".

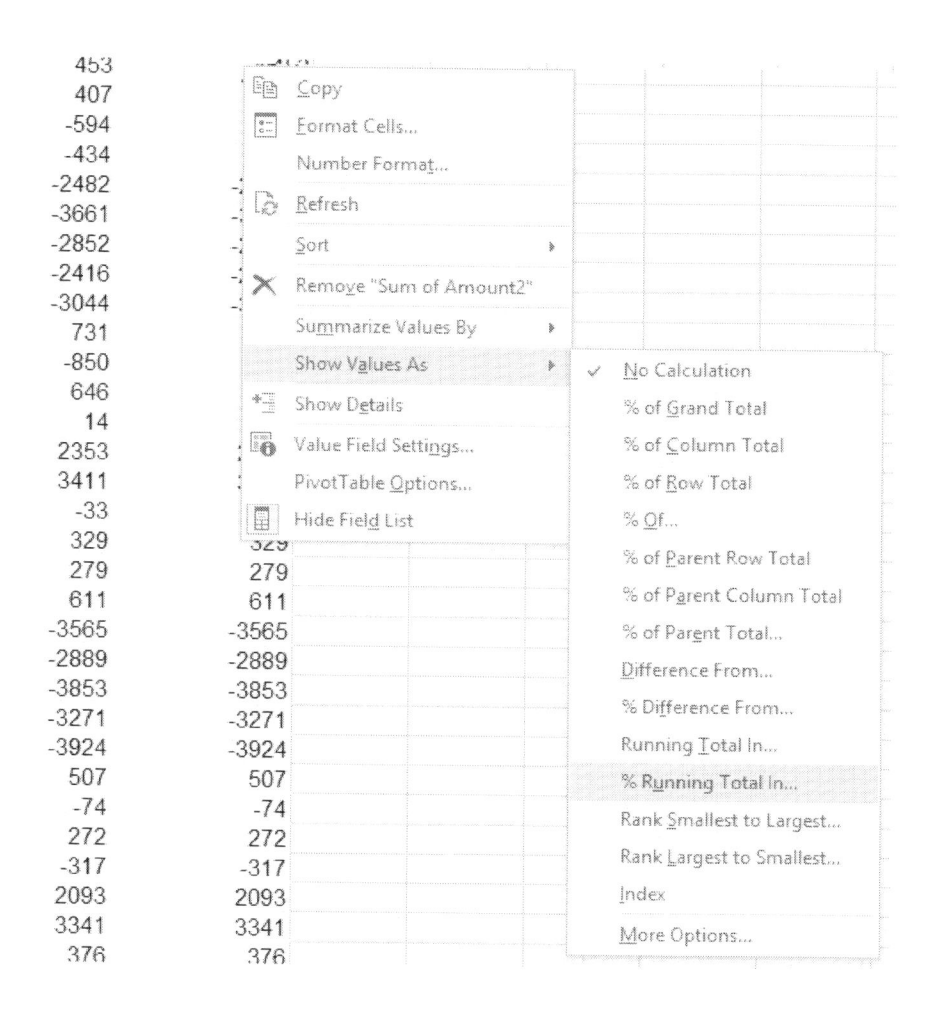

Select the field that will be used as a cumulative basis (the date field):

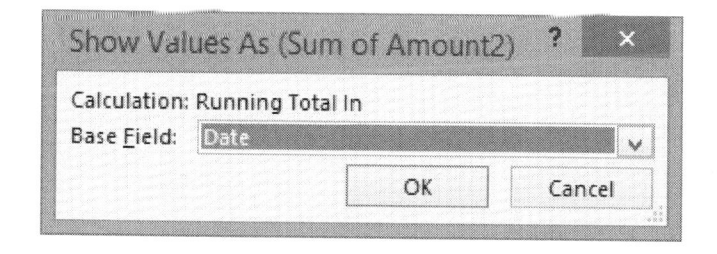

The following pivot table will appear:

Row Labels	Sum of Amount	Sum of Amount2
1/2/2012	453	453
1/5/2012	407	860
1/8/2012	-594	266
1/11/2012	-434	-168
1/14/2012	-2482	-2650
1/17/2012	-3661	-6311
1/20/2012	-2852	-9163
1/23/2012	-2416	-11579
1/26/2012	-3044	-14623
1/29/2012	731	-13892
2/1/2012	-850	-14742
2/4/2012	646	-14096
2/7/2012	14	-14082
2/10/2012	2353	-11729
2/13/2012	3411	-8318
2/16/2012	-33	-8351
2/19/2012	329	-8022
2/22/2012	279	-7743
2/25/2012	611	-7132

This table shows, for example, that on 02/09/2012, an amount of 329 USD was obtained and the accrued balance for that date is (-8022) USD.

Percentage of

One of the more interesting options we have is to display the data compared to other given data.

We have created a pivot table that displays the average salaries, sorted by city.

We dragged the salary field to the values area twice, and changed the calculation to average.

City	Average of Monthly Salary	Average of Monthly Salary2
Detroit	2,457.78	2,457.78
Los Angeles	2,495.83	2,495.83
Miami	2,562.96	2,562.96
New Jersey	2,472.26	2,472.26
New York	2,359.98	2,359.98
San Diego	2,629.10	2,629.10
Grand Total	2,504.88	2,504.88

Now we want to see the average monthly salary compared to New Jersey.

In the second salary field, select "**% of**."

In the new window, we are asked to select the base field (the City field) and the item in the field (New Jersey):

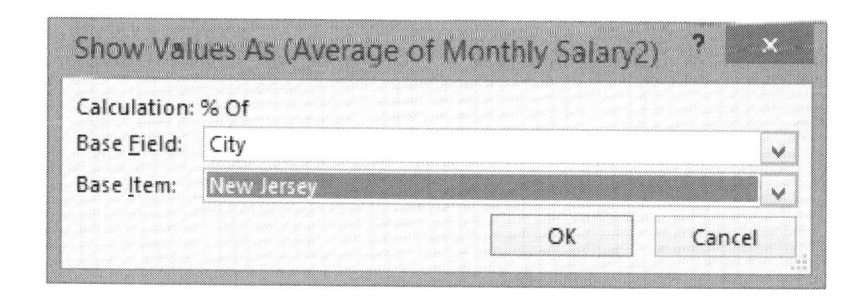

Show Values As (Average of Monthly Salary2)

Calculation: % Of
Base Field: City
Base Item: New Jersey

OK   Cancel

The following pivot table is created:

City	Average of Monthly Salary	Average of Monthly Salary2
Detroit	2458	99.41%
Los Angeles	2496	100.95%
Miami	2563	103.67%
New Jersey	2472	100.00%
New York	2360	95.46%
San Diego	2629	106.34%
Grand Total	2505	

We can see that the city New Jersey constitutes the basis, and thus is displayed as 100%, while other cities are presented in comparison to it.

You can see, for example, that the average salary in Detroit is 99.41% of the average salary in New Jersey (i.e., about 0.6% lower), while the average salary in Miami is about 3% higher.

Data Grouping

A pivot table enables us to group data in various ways.

We may group:

- Numeric data, e.g. grouping height data at intervals of 2 inches
- Dates, e.g. displaying the dates of birth, grouped by months
- Textual data

Grouping numeric data

In the following example, we have created a pivot table that shows the number of people who earn a certain salary:

Monthly Salary	Count of Employee No.
$ 1,651.00	3
$ 1,652.00	2
$ 1,653.00	3
$ 1,654.00	2
$ 1,655.00	1
$ 1,656.00	2
$ 1,657.00	2
$ 1,659.00	2
$ 1,662.00	3
$ 1,663.00	2
$ 1,664.00	3
$ 1,665.00	1
$ 1,666.00	5
$ 1,667.00	1
$ 1,670.00	4

Using the above example, we can see that 3 employees earn a monthly salary of 1,651 USD while other employees earn greater salaries.

Although the data is correct, it is actually meaningless until we group it:

1. Place the cursor on the pivot table, in one of the cells that contains the salary data.

2. Under the "**ANALYZE**" tab, select "**Group Field**", or simply right-click an item in the salary field, and select "**Group**":

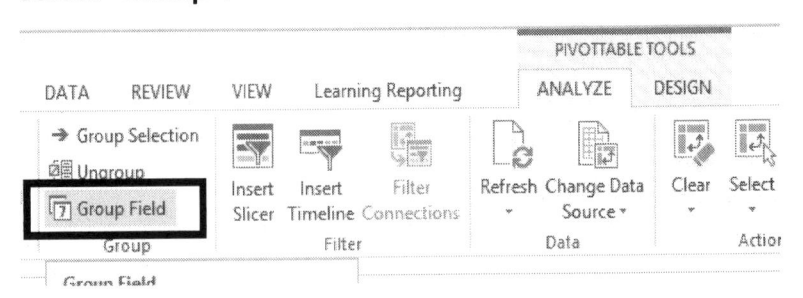

3. The following window will appear:

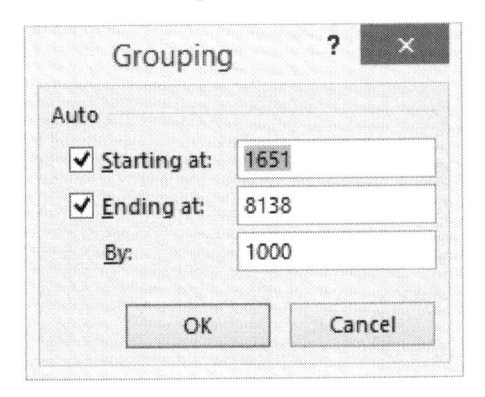

By default, the lowest value is displayed as the "**Starting** at" and the highest value is displayed as the "**Ending at**" value, but we can change the values as we wish, as shown in the following window:

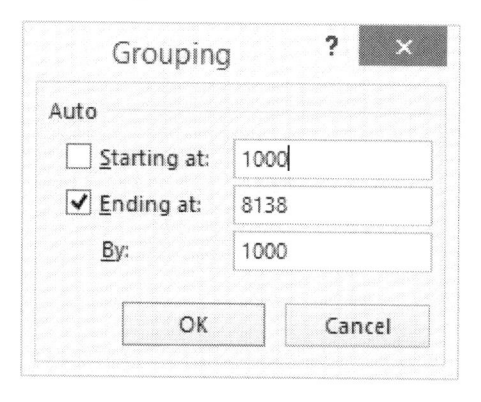

[Grouping dialog box: Auto, Starting at: 1000, Ending at: 8138, By: 1000, OK, Cancel]

4. Select the units or intervals by which you wish to group the data (in this case, we selected grouping by 1000 USD intervals).

5. Click OK

6. The pivot table will look like the one below:

Monthly Salary	Count of Employee No.
1000-1999	713
2000-2999	27
3000-3999	116
4000-4999	111
5000-5999	1
6000-6999	8
7000-7999	20
8000-8999	4
Grand Total	1000

We can now see, for example, that 27 employees earn monthly salaries ranging from 2000 to 2999 USD.

Date Grouping

In the following example, we sought to examine the number of people (identified by their ID) hired to work on each date.

The following table appears:

Row Labels	Count of Emp Name
1/6/2011	1
1/7/2011	2
1/8/2011	2
1/10/2011	4
1/11/2011	1
1/12/2011	4
1/14/2011	1
1/15/2011	2
1/17/2011	2
1/18/2011	2
1/20/2011	1
1/21/2011	2
1/23/2011	4
1/24/2011	3
1/25/2011	1
1/26/2011	3
1/27/2011	4

To facilitate our understanding, we need to group the data so we can see the number of people hired each month:

1. Place the cursor on the pivot table in one of the cells that contains a date.

2. Under the " **ANALYZE**" tab, select "**Group Field**" (you can also right click on an item in the dates field ⟶ **Group**):

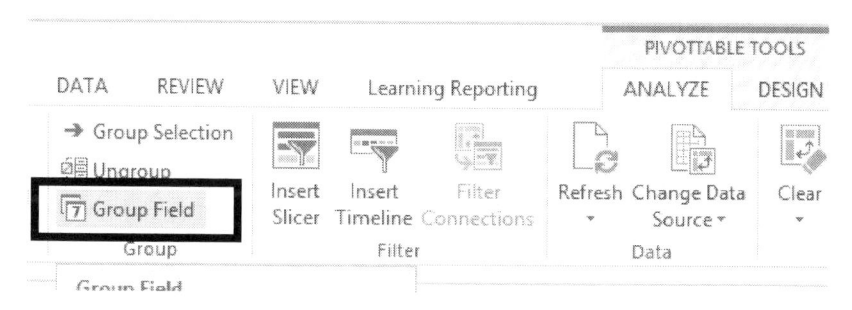

3. The following window will appear:

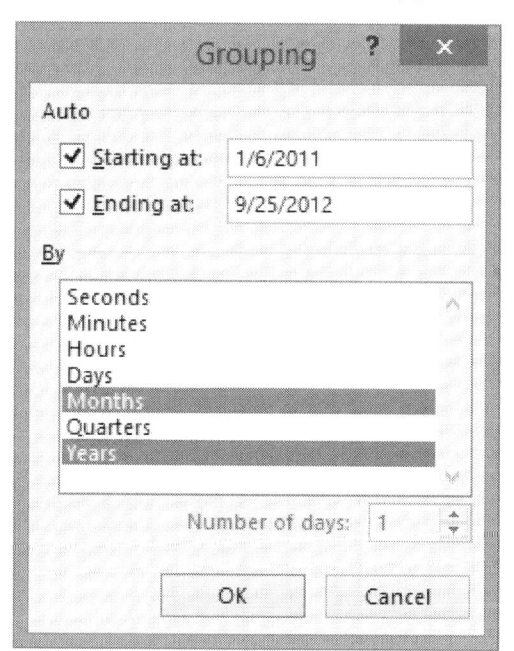

4. Select the desired options for grouping:

Years	Hire Date	Count of Emp Name
⊟ 2011	Jan	46
	Feb	40
	Mar	55
	Apr	65
	May	50
	Jun	74
	Jul	81
	Aug	50
	Sep	23
	Oct	18
	Nov	47
	Dec	39
⊟ 2012	Jan	59
	Feb	47
	Mar	63
	Apr	66
	May	91
	Jun	48
	Jul	20
	Aug	15
	Sep	3
Grand Total		1000

Please note that you should select not only months, but also years; otherwise, the report will show the number of people hired to work each month, regardless of the year of acceptance. For example, employees hired in January 2001 will appear in the same row as employees hired in January 2002.

Grouping textual data

As seen above, it is easy to group numeric data or dates. However, it frequently becomes necessary to group textual data.

The text grouping is done manually, as explained below:

1. In the pivot table select the data you would like to group. In this example, we want to create a group of managers, so we select the manager and the department manager:

Role	Average of Monthly Salary
Accountant	4551.00
Bookkeeper	2773.20
Department Manager	4730.33
Engineer	7474.41
Manager	3996.67
Person Marketing	3095.00
Practical Engineer	7384.80
Production Worker	1827.39
Recruitment Coordinator	1843.00
salesperson	3998.59
Senior Recruitment Coordinator	4737.33
Grand Total	2504.88

Note: sequential data can be selected by dragging. Non-sequential data can be selected by using the Ctrl key.

2. In the "**ANALYZE**" tab, under "**PIVOTTABLE TOOLS**", select "**Group Selection**":

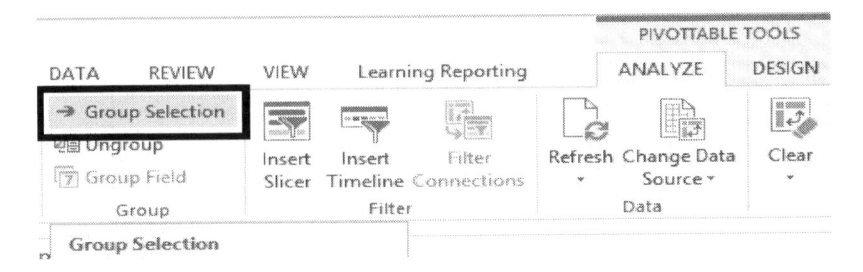

3. A new group appears, which contains the two groups selected before:

Role2	Role	Average of Monthly Salary
⊟ Accountant	Accountant	4551.00
⊟ Bookkeeper	Bookkeeper	2773.20
⊟ Group1	Department Manager	4730.33
	Manager	3996.67
⊟ Engineer	Engineer	7474.44
⊟ Person Marketing	Person Marketing	3095.00
⊟ Practical Engineer	Practical Engineer	7384.80
⊟ Production Worker	Production Worker	1827.39
⊟ Recruitment Coordinator	Recruitment Coordinator	1843.00
⊟ salesperson	salesperson	3998.59
⊟ Senior Recruitment Coordinato	Senior Recruitment Coordinator	4737.33
Grand Total		2504.88

4. If we choose to present the subtotals as well, we can see that the two groups are merged into one:

Role2	Role	Average of Monthly Salary
⊟ Accountant	Accountant	4551.00
Accountant Total		4551.00
⊟ Bookkeeper	Bookkeeper	2773.20
Bookkeeper Total		2773.20
⊟ Group1	Department Manager	4730.33
	Manager	3996.67
Group1 Total		4241.22
⊟ Engineer	Engineer	7474.41
Engineer Total		7474.41
⊟ Person Marketing	Person Marketing	3095.00
Person Marketing Total		3095.00
⊟ Practical Engineer	Practical Engineer	7384.80
Practical Engineer Total		7384.80
⊟ Production Worker	Production Worker	1827.39
Production Worker Total		1827.39
⊟ Recruitment Coordinator	Recruitment Coordinator	1843.00
Recruitment Coordinator Total		1843.00
⊟ salesperson	salesperson	3998.59
salesperson Total		3998.59
⊟ Senior Recruitment Coordinato	Senior Recruitment Coordinator	4737.33
Senior Recruitment Coordinator Total		4737.33
Grand Total		2504.88

Multivalued Report

Every now and then we need to perform a large number of calculations for the same field, e.g. calculation of minimum, maximum and average salary.

We can drag the salary field onto the VALUES area several times, and change the calculation type for each one.

In the following example, we dragged the salary field into the VALUES area four times:

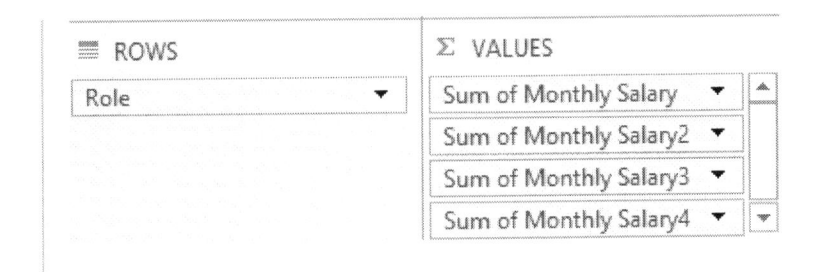

```
≡ ROWS                          Σ VALUES
┌─────────────────────┐         ┌──────────────────────────┐
│ Role              ▼ │         │ Sum of Monthly Salary  ▼ │
└─────────────────────┘         │ Sum of Monthly Salary2 ▼ │
                                │ Sum of Monthly Salary3 ▼ │
                                │ Sum of Monthly Salary4 ▼ │
                                └──────────────────────────┘
```

The following pivot table appeared:

Role	Sum of Monthly Salary	Sum of Monthly Salary2	Sum of Monthly Salary3	Sum of Monthly Salary4
Accountant	13653.00	13653.00	13653.00	13653.00
Bookkeeper	13866.00	13866.00	13866.00	13866.00
Department Manager	14191.00	14191.00	14191.00	14191.00
Engineer	127065.00	127065.00	127065.00	127065.00
Manager	23980.00	23980.00	23980.00	23980.00
Person Marketing	34045.00	34045.00	34045.00	34045.00
Practical Engineer	110772.00	110772.00	110772.00	110772.00
Production Worker	1332167.00	1332167.00	1332167.00	1332167.00
Recruitment Coordinator	9215.00	9215.00	9215.00	9215.00
salesperson	811713.00	811713.00	811713.00	811713.00
Senior Recruitment Coordinator	14212.00	14212.00	14212.00	14212.00
Grand Total	2504879.00	2504879.00	2504879.00	2504879.00

Now, all that remains is to change the calculation for each column, as we learned in the "**Changing Calculations**" section on page 41. This creates the following pivot table:

Role	Count of Monthly Salary	Average of Monthly Salary2	Max of Monthly Salary3	Min of Monthly Salary4
Accountant	3.00	4551.00	4841.00	4285.00
Bookkeeper	5.00	2773.20	3107.00	2617.00
Department Manager	3.00	4730.33	5140.00	4449.00
Engineer	17.00	7474.41	8138.00	6725.00
Manager	6.00	3996.67	4304.00	3820.00
Person Marketing	11.00	3095.00	3346.00	2864.00
Practical Engineer	15.00	7384.80	7888.00	6666.00
Production Worker	729.00	1827.39	2016.00	1651.00
Recruitment Coordinator	5.00	1843.00	2015.00	1727.00
salesperson	203.00	3998.59	4399.00	3613.00
Senior Recruitment Coordinator	3.00	4737.33	4850.00	4557.00
Grand Total	1000.00	2504.88	8138.00	1651.00

Calculated Field

A calculated field enables us to perform calculations between different fields of the pivot table, or between a field and a constant.

Calculation based on a single field

One example of this is a tax calculation. We could add a column that calculates the tax in the data table itself, or we can add it directly to the pivot table. This form of calculation is especially effective when using data from external tables (for example – Access or SQL) and not from our current Excel file.

It also saves memory, since the calculation is performed on grouped data, and not for each record in the database.

1. Place the cursor on the pivot table.
2. Select the "**ANALYZE**" tab.
3. Select "**Fields, Items and Sets**".

4. Select "**Calculated Field**":

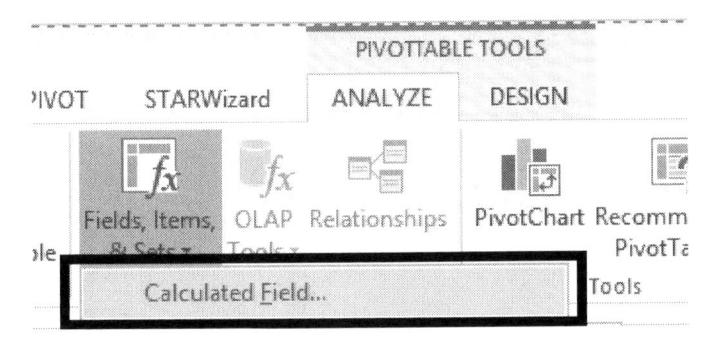

The following window will appear:

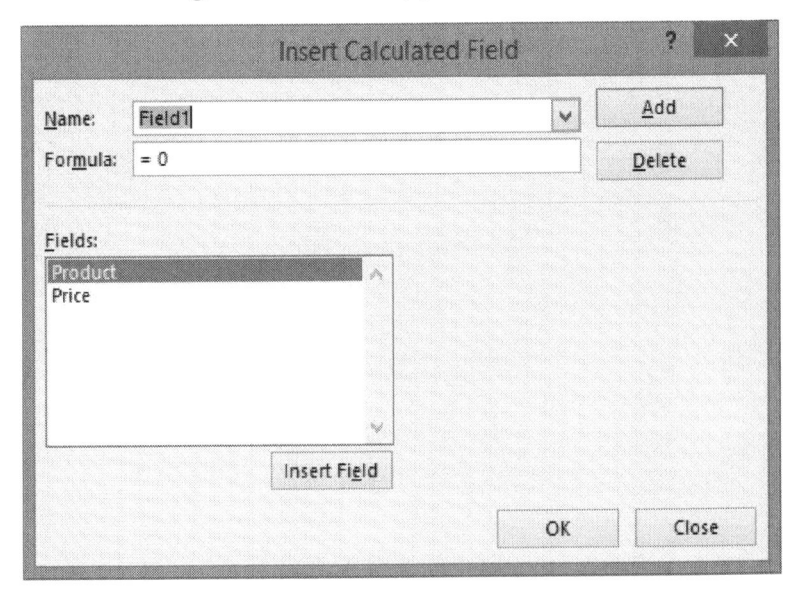

   a. Name the field.

   b. Select the field in which the calculation will be performed.

   c. Click the `Insert Field` button.

d. Continue to create the formula:

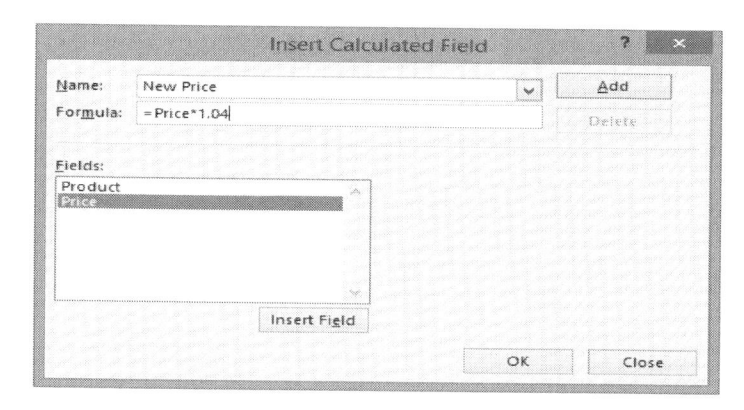

```
Insert Calculated Field
Name:     New Price                          Add
Formula:  =Price*1.04                        Delete

Fields:
Product
Price

                    Insert Field
                                     OK      Close
```

e. Click [OK]

The pivot table will look like this:

Row Labels	Sum of Price	Sum of New Price
computer	325	338
keyboard	19.99	20.7896
Mouse	14.99	15.5896
Grand Total	359.98	374.3792

Calculation based on several fields in a pivot table

We may sometimes need to perform a calculation based on several fields in a pivot table.

The following example is inventory management, based on a table containing data about the numbers of ingoing and outgoing products:

date	SKU	In	Out
3/11/2014	8	4	1
3/12/2014	9	4	1
3/13/2014	5	2	2
3/14/2014	1	1	2
3/15/2014	3	1	2
3/16/2014	9	3	2
3/17/2014	2	4	5
3/18/2014	6	4	4
3/11/2014	9	1	3
3/12/2014	3	5	1
3/13/2014	5	4	2
3/14/2014	8	5	1
3/15/2014	8	1	2
3/16/2014	10	1	2
3/17/2014	4	1	3
3/18/2014	6	3	5
3/11/2014	3	1	4
3/12/2014	7	3	2
3/13/2014	5	3	5
3/14/2014	2	4	2

We want to create a report that will display the difference between the incoming and the outgoing inventory for each SKU, across all dates.

The first step is to create a pivot table that contains the data of incoming and outgoing inventory for each SKU:

SKU	Sum of In	Sum of Out
1	6	4
2	16	17
3	13	12
4	7	11
5	21	17
6	11	15
7	20	16
8	12	9
9	11	7
10	1	2
Grand Total	118	110

To create the calculated field:

1. Place the cursor on the pivot table.
2. Select the "**ANALYZE**" tab.
3. Select "**Fields, Items and Sets**".
4. Select "**Calculated Field**":

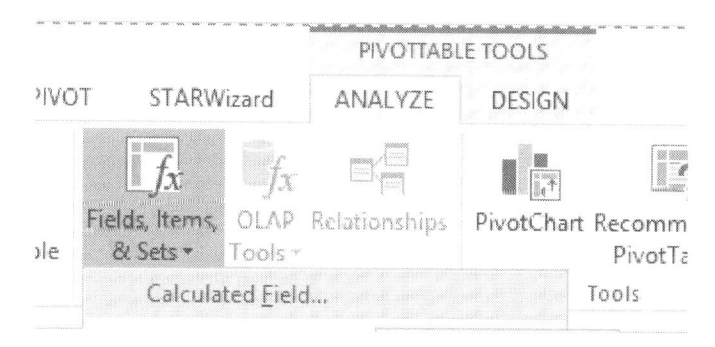

The following window will appear:

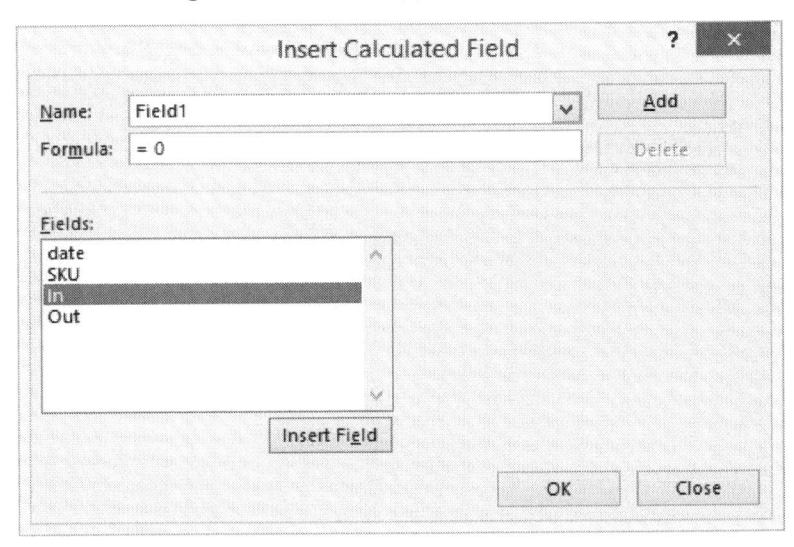

```
Insert Calculated Field                    ?  ×

Name:    Field1                    ∨     Add
Formula: = 0                             Delete

Fields:
date
SKU
In
Out

           Insert Field

                              OK         Close
```

a. Name the field.

b. Select the field involved in the calculation.

c. Click the **Insert Field** button.

d. Type the arithmetic operations (add/multiply etc.).

e. Select the second relevant field.

f. Click the **Insert Field** button.

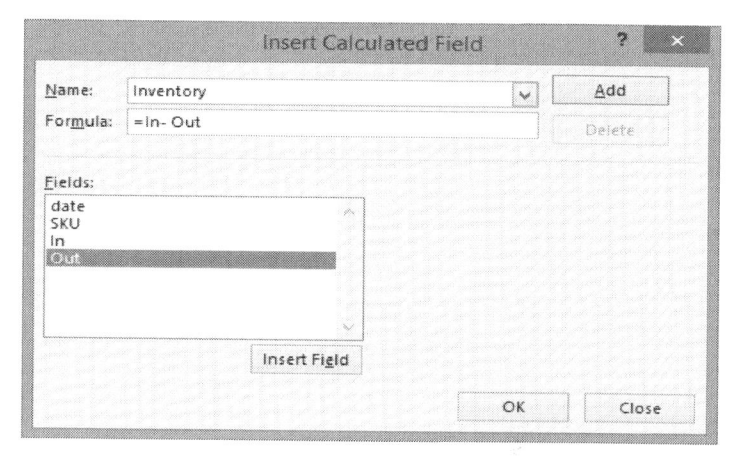

[Dialog box: Insert Calculated Field — Name: Inventory; Formula: =In- Out; Fields: date, SKU, In, Out (Out selected)]

g. Press OK.

5. The following table will appear:

Row Labels	Sum of In	Sum of Out	Sum of Inventory
1	6	4	2
2	16	17	-1
3	13	12	1
4	7	11	-4
5	21	17	4
6	11	15	-4
7	20	16	4
8	12	9	3
9	11	7	4
10	1	2	-1
Grand Total	118	110	8

Deleting a calculated field

To delete a calculated field, select it from the drop-down list and click "Delete"

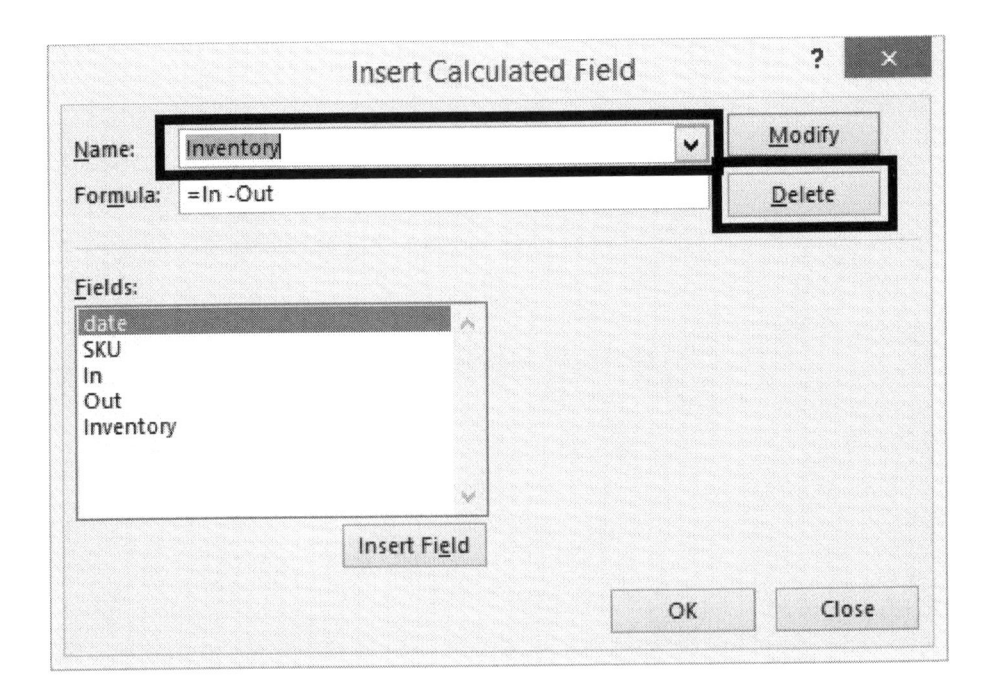

[Screenshot of "Insert Calculated Field" dialog box with Name: Inventory, Formula: =In -Out, Fields list showing date, SKU, In, Out, Inventory, and buttons Modify, Delete, Insert Field, OK, Close.]

Please note that the calculated field should not be directly removed from the pivot table areas!

Calculated Item

"Calculated Item" enables us to perform calculations within a field (as opposed to "Calculated field", which enables us to perform calculations between fields). In other words, the calculation is performed between the different items of the field.

As an example, we can use the inventory table from page 68. Remember that the table had two columns representing the inventory; one column for incoming inventory and another column for outgoing inventory. However, information can be organized differently. Instead of two columns, we can combine the two fields in one column, and add a "Direction" field, so that the data table will look like the following:

Date	SKU	Qty	Direction
3/11/2014	9	2	In
3/12/2014	6	1	Out
3/13/2014	2	3	In
3/14/2014	10	2	Out
3/15/2014	10	2	In
3/16/2014	7	5	Out
3/17/2014	10	3	In
3/18/2014	8	4	Out
3/11/2014	7	3	In
3/12/2014	3	4	Out
3/13/2014	6	3	In
3/14/2014	7	3	Out
3/15/2014	8	3	In
3/16/2014	2	5	Out
3/17/2014	6	4	In
3/18/2014	7	3	Out
3/11/2014	9	2	In

In this case, contrary to the "Calculated field", which is performed between the two fields, we seek to make a calculation on items in the same field. That is, to subtract the outgoing items of inventory from the incoming items, using the "Direction" field.

1. From the data above, create a pivot table like the following:

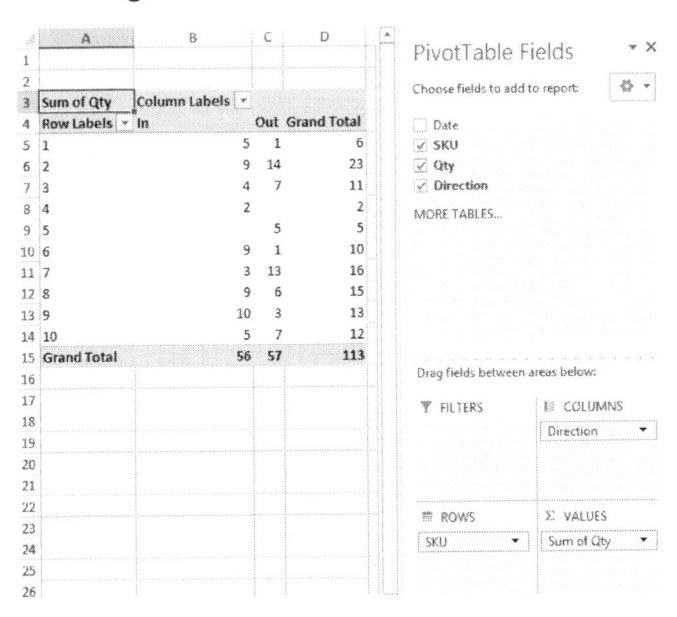

2. Cancel the Grand Total which, in this case, displays an incorrect result (due to the data structure, the incoming and outgoing data should be subtracted and not added).

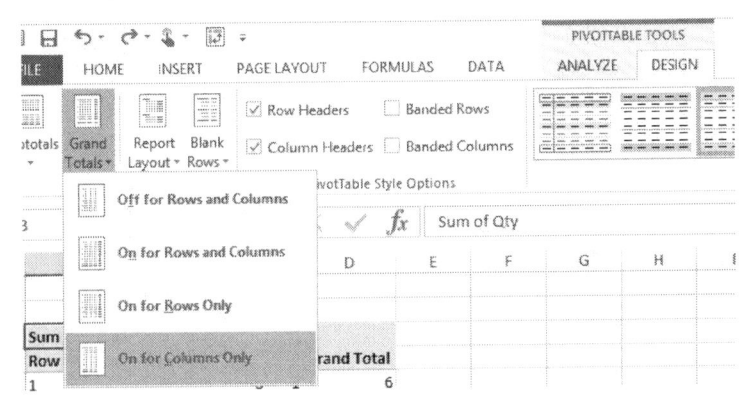

3. Place the cursor on one of the title fields designated for calculation ("In" or "Out").

4. Select **"Fields, Items and Sets"** ⟶ **"Calculated Item"**:

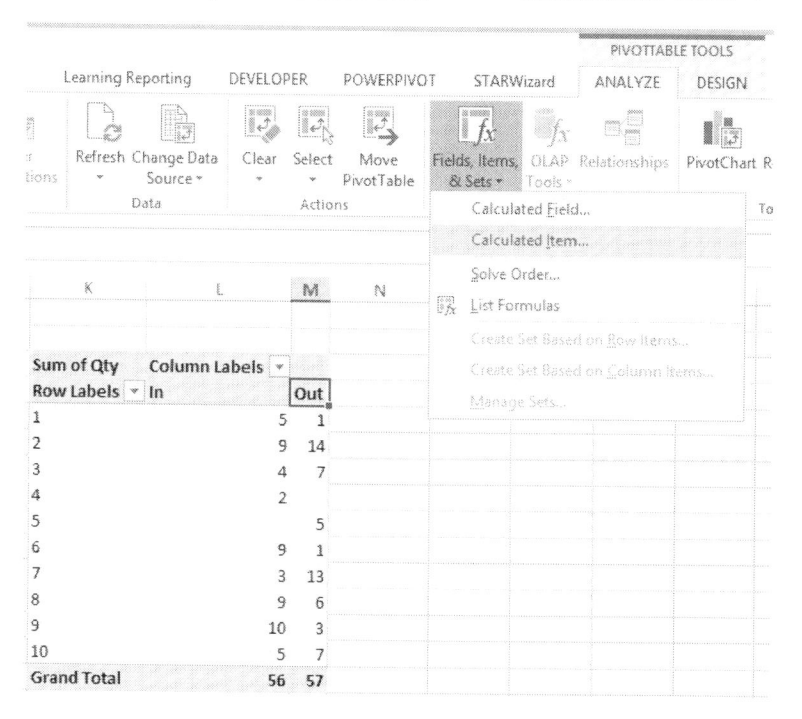

5. Construct the formula:

    a. In the name field, type a meaningful name (e.g. "Inventory").

    b. In the name field, type a meaningful name (e.g. "Inventory").

    c. Select the "Direction" field, on the left-hand side of the screen.

d. Items of "Direction" will appear on the right-hand side of the screen, as can be seen in the following figure:

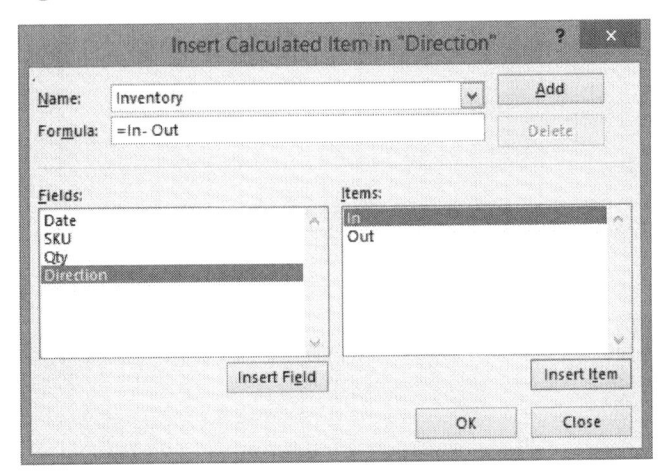

> **Insert Calculated Item in "Direction"**
>
> Name: Inventory
> Formula: =In- Out
>
> Fields:
> Date
> SKU
> Qty
> Direction
>
> Items:
> In
> Out
>
> [Insert Field] [Insert Item]
> [OK] [Close]
> [Add] [Delete]

e. Build the formula by using items (items are data within a field):

f. Select the first item and then "Insert Item" (in our example, select "In").

g. Type the desired action (in our example, subtraction).

h. Select the second item and then "Insert Item" (in our example, select "Out").

i. The formula will appear at the top of the screen, as shown in the following figure:

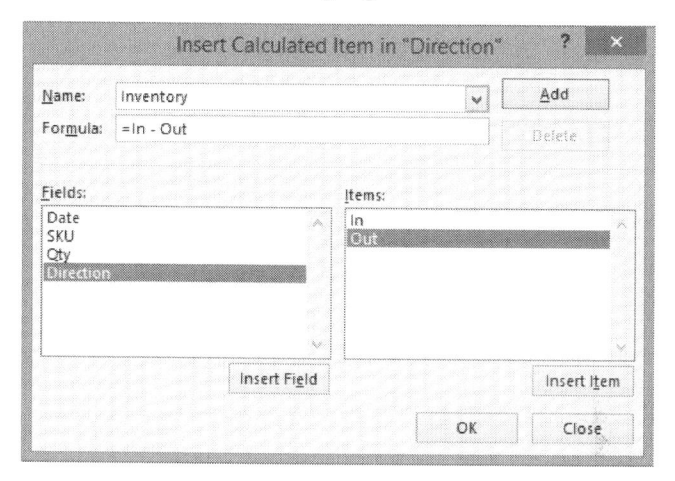

j. Click OK

6. The following pivot table will appear; it includes the difference between the incoming and outgoing inventory for each SKU:

Sum of Qty	Column Labels		
Row Labels	In	Out	Inventory
1	5	1	4
2	9	14	-5
3	4	7	-3
4	2		2
5		5	-5
6	9	1	8
7	3	13	-10
8	9	6	3
9	10	3	7
10	5	7	-2
Grand Total	56	57	-1

Note that the item name is a component in the formula of the calculated item. Therefore, changing the item names in the data table (for example, replacing "Inventory" with "Inventory Income") may affect the result of the calculated item in the pivot table.

Exercises

1. Display the number of cars by desired price. Display the quantity grouped to units of 500 USD.

2. Display the average desired price by engine capacity. Change it to maximum price by engine capacity.

3. Display the number of cars by date of sale. Group the dates by years, quarters and months.

4. Display the average desired price by make. Group the Japanese cars only (Subaru and Suzuki).

5. Display the average, minimum and maximum price, by gear type.

6. Display the sum of sales by gear type.

7. Add tax (4%) to the sale price of the previous report using Calculated Field.

8. Display the amount of the desired price by publication date. Add a column and calculate the running total by publication date.

9. Create a report that displays the country of manufacture in the ROWS, the type of gear in the COLUMN and the number of cars (counting) in the VALUES.

   Display the difference between the number of cars with automatic gears and the number of cars with manual gears, using Calculated Item.

Changing the Report Structure

The pivot table enables us to make changes in the report structure. The changes will be displayed immediately by:

- Switching between columns and rows
- Inserting columns or rows

Switching columns and rows

When creating a report, the locations of fields can be changed by dragging them to a different area.

In the following example, we created a pivot table that shows the average monthly salary for each city and role:

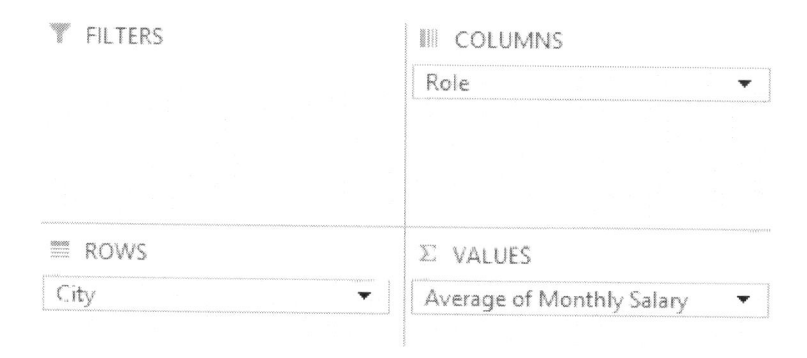

▼ FILTERS	▥ COLUMNS
	Role ▼

≡ ROWS	Σ VALUES
City ▼	Average of Monthly Salary ▼

The following table appears:

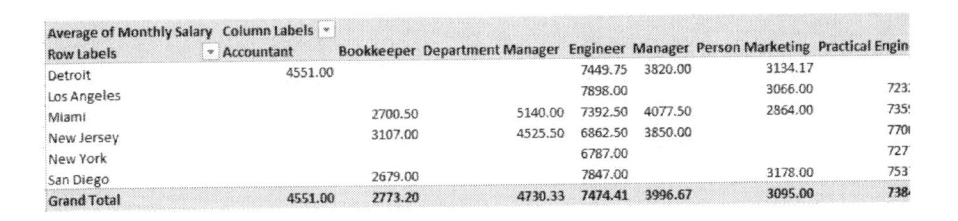

Average of Monthly Salary	Column Labels						
Row Labels	Accountant	Bookkeeper	Department Manager	Engineer	Manager	Person Marketing	Practical Engin
Detroit	4551.00			7449.75	3820.00	3134.17	
Los Angeles				7898.00		3066.00	723.
Miami		2700.50	5140.00	7392.50	4077.50	2864.00	735!
New Jersey		3107.00	4525.50	6862.50	3850.00		770(
New York				6787.00			727
San Diego		2679.00		7847.00		3178.00	753
Grand Total	4551.00	2773.20	4730.33	7474.41	3996.67	3095.00	738.

However, since the number of cities is small compared to the large number of roles, reading the data becomes quite difficult. To make it clearer, we can switch the rows and columns of the pivot table around.

All we have to do is to drag the "Role" field to the COLUMNS and the "City" field to the ROWS:

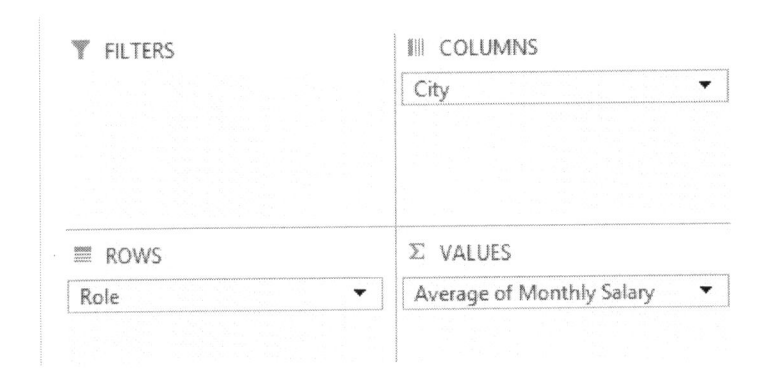

FILTERS

COLUMNS
City

ROWS
Role

Σ VALUES
Average of Monthly Salary

The following pivot table will appear:

Average of Monthly Salary	Column Labels						
Row Labels	Detroit	Los Angeles	Miami	New Jersey	New York	San Diego	Grand Total
Accountant	4551.00						4551.00
Bookkeeper			2700.50	3107.00		2679.00	2773.20
Department Manager			5140.00	4525.50			4730.33
Engineer	7449.75	7898.00	7392.50	6862.50	6787.00	7847.00	7474.41
Manager	3820.00		4077.50	3850.00			3996.67
Person Marketing	3134.17	3066.00	2864.00			3178.00	3095.00
Practical Engineer		7232.75	7359.00	7700.00	7277.00	7537.75	7384.80
Production Worker	1830.06	1837.78	1827.98	1818.48	1814.56	1825.28	1827.39
Recruitment Coordinator	1882.00	1736.50	1845.00		2015.00		1843.00
salesperson	4011.44	3982.03	3918.35	4034.56	3767.67	4048.43	3998.59
Senior Recruitment Coordinator	4805.00		4850.00	4557.00			4737.33
Grand Total	2457.78	2495.83	2562.96	2472.26	2359.98	2629.10	2504.88

Note that both tables display the same data. Select the one which is more readable for you.

Adding columns or rows

1. Additional columns or rows can be easily added to the report by dragging the appropriate fields to the COLUMNS or ROWS.

In this example, we added the "Gender" field to the ROWS, below the "Role" field:

≡ ROWS
Role
Gender

The following table displays the average salary in each city, divided by role, then gender:

83

Average of Monthly Salary	Column Labels						
Row Labels	Detroit	Los Angeles	Miami	New Jersey	New York	San Diego	Grand Total
⊟ Accountant	4551.00						4551.00
Female	4563.00						4563.00
Male	4527.00						4527.00
⊟ Bookkeeper			2700.50	3107.00		2679.00	2773.20
Female			2746.00	3107.00		2741.00	2864.67
Male			2655.00			2617.00	2636.00
⊟ Department Manager			5140.00	4525.50			4730.33
Female			5140.00	4449.00			4794.50
Male				4602.00			4602.00
⊟ Engineer	7449.75	7898.00	7392.50	6862.50	6787.00	7847.00	7474.41
Female	7449.75	7898.00					7599.17
Male			7392.50	6862.50	6787.00	7847.00	7406.36
⊟ Manager	3820.00		4077.50	3850.00			3996.67

Within the ROWS area, we can drag the "Role" field below the "Gender" field.

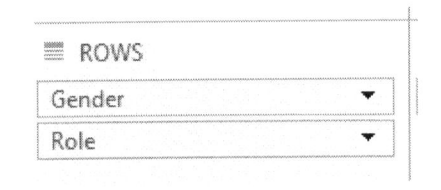

≡ ROWS

Gender ▼
Role ▼

We get the following pivot table, which displays the average salary in each city, divided by gender, then role:

Average of Monthly Salary	Column Labels						
Row Labels	Detroit	Los Angeles	Miami	New Jersey	New York	San Diego	Grand Total
Female							
Accountant	4,563.0						4,563.0
Bookkeeper			2,746.0	3,107.0		2,741.0	2,864.7
Department Manager			5,140.0	4,449.0			4,794.5
Engineer	7,449.8	7,898.0					7,599.2
Manager	3,820.0						3,820.0
Person Marketing	3,134.2	3,066.0					3,111.4
Practical Engineer		7,232.8					7,232.8
Production Worker	1,831.7	1,841.1	1,795.8	1,823.2	1,813.5	1,865.8	1,833.0
Recruitment Coordinator	1,882.0	1,736.5					1,785.0
Salesperson	4,012.9	3,993.5	4,306.0	4,010.0	4,199.0	4,322.0	4,015.1
Senior Recruitment Coordinator	4,805.0						4,805.0
Male							
Accountant	4,527.0						4,527.0
Bookkeeper			2,655.0			2,617.0	2,636.0
Department Manager				4,602.0			4,602.0
Engineer			7,392.5	6,862.5	6,787.0	7,847.0	7,406.4
Manager			4,077.5	3,850.0			4,032.0
Person Marketing			2,864.0			3,178.0	3,021.0
Practical Engineer			7,359.0	7,700.0	7,277.0	7,537.8	7,440.1
Production Worker	1,811.5	1,819.2	1,834.0	1,817.6	1,814.7	1,819.6	1,821.9
Recruitment Coordinator			1,845.0		2,015.0		1,930.0
Salesperson	3,906.0	3,662.0	3,902.8	4,038.5	3,681.4	4,040.4	3,980.5
Senior Recruitment Coordinator			4,850.0	4,557.0			4,703.5
Grand Total	**2,457.8**	**2,495.8**	**2,563.0**	**2,472.3**	**2,360.0**	**2,629.1**	**2,504.9**

Adding a page break between items

We may sometimes need to print each item of the pivot table on a separate page. Such a need arises, for example, if the department manager requires only the details of their own department.

To insert a page break between items, follow these steps:

1. Create a pivot table with at least two fields in the ROWS ("Department" and "Role", for example).

2. Place the cursor on the upper field (in our case, "Department"), and press the arrow.

3. Click on "**Field Settings**":

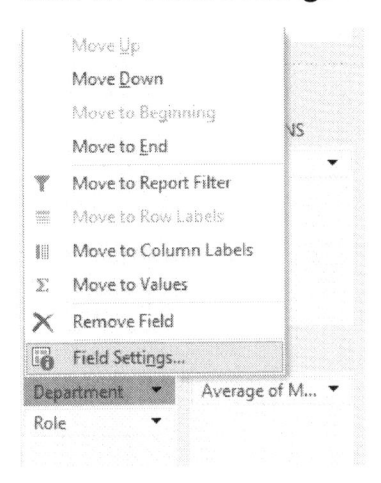

4. Select "**Layout and Print**" tab.

5. Check the "**Insert page break after each item**" box:

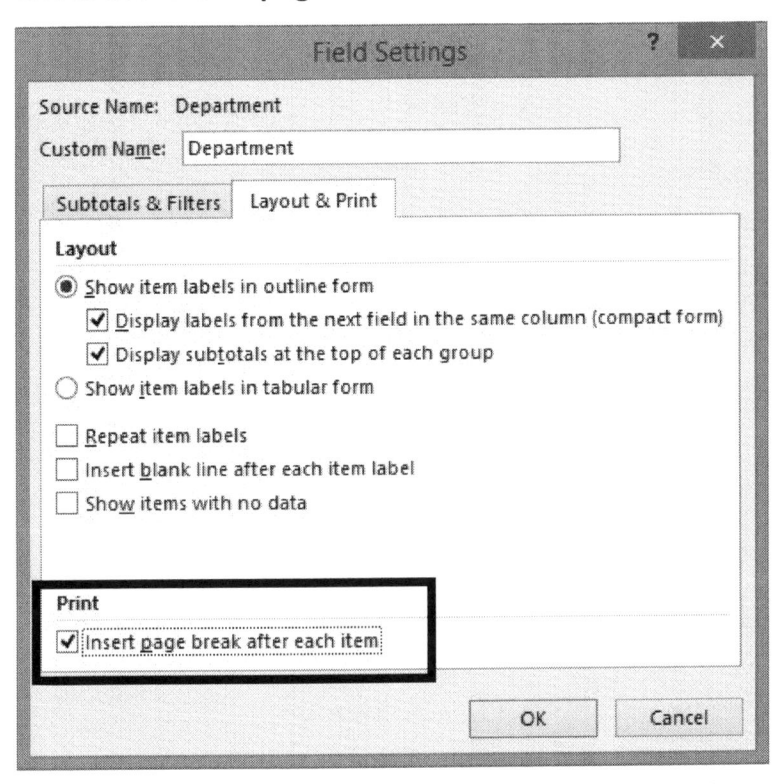

6. At the second stage, go to the "**PAGE LAYOUT**" tab → "**Print Titles**":

7. Select the table titles as "**Rows to repeat at top**":

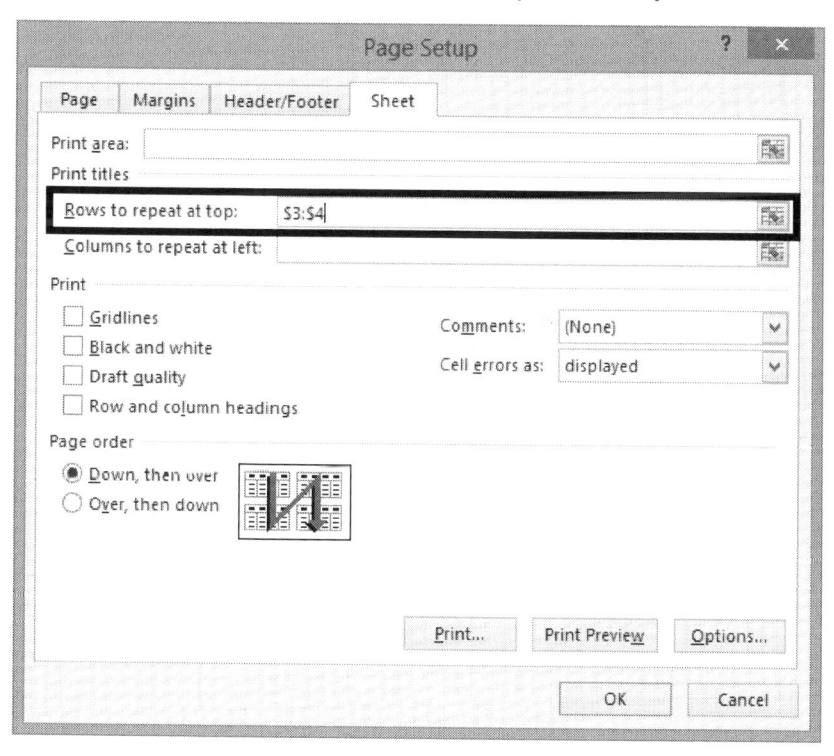

Now, the data for each department will be printed on a separate page.

Exercises

1. Create a pivot table report displaying the car color in the ROWS and the gear type in the COLUMNS. Calculate the average desired price.

2. Switch the ROWS and COLUMNS.

3. Create a pivot table report displaying the car color in the ROWS and the country of manufacture in the COLUMNS. Calculate the number of cars.

4. Switch the ROWS and COLUMNS.

Formatting Pivot Tables

Structure Format

Pivot tables have format defaults, set by the software. However, we can customize the tables according to our needs.

Subtotals

If the pivot table has at least 2 fields in the ROWS or in the COLUMNS, data in the pivot table will appear with subtotals after each change of an item in a field, as shown in the following figure:

Section	City	Gender	Average of Monthly Salary
Management	Detroit	Female	3927
		Male	4527
	Detroit Total		**4027**
	Los Angeles	Female	1737
	Los Angeles Total		1737
	Miami	Female	3943
		Male	3315
	Miami Total		3524
	New Jersey	Female	3107
		Male	4557
	New Jersey Total		3832
	New York	Male	2015
	New York Total		2015
	San Diego	Female	2741
		Male	2617
	San Diego Total		2679
Management Total			3359
Manufacturing	Detroit	Female	1937
		Male	1812
	Detroit Total		1927
	Los Angeles	Female	2178
		Male	1819

Subtotal format:

We can format the subtotals in order to distinguish more easily between them and the data.

Formatting can be done by cell color, font color, highlights, font size, etc.:

- Place the cursor in the total row, on one of the titles. In our example, you can place the cursor on "Detroit Total".
- Move the cursor to the left until it turns from the ✧ shape to the ➡ shape.
- The entire total row is now selected, as shown in the following figure:

Section	City	Gender	Average of Monthly Salary
Management	Detroit	Female	3927
		Male	4527
	Detroit Total		**4027**
	Los Angeles	Female	1737
	Los Angeles Total		**1737**
	Miami	Female	3943
		Male	3315
	Miami Total		**3524**
	New Jersey	Female	3107
		Male	4557
	New Jersey Total		**3832**
	New York	Male	2015
	New York Total		**2015**
	San Diego	Female	2741
		Male	2617
	San Diego Total		**2679**
Management Total			3359
Manufacturing	Detroit	Female	1937
		Male	1812
	Detroit Total		**1927**
	Los Angeles	Female	2178
		Male	1819

- The cells can now be formatted as we wish (cell filling, color, size, etc.).

Removing or Changing the subtotals location:

1. Place the cursor on the pivot table.
2. Select the "**DESIGN**" tab ⟶ "**Subtotals**":

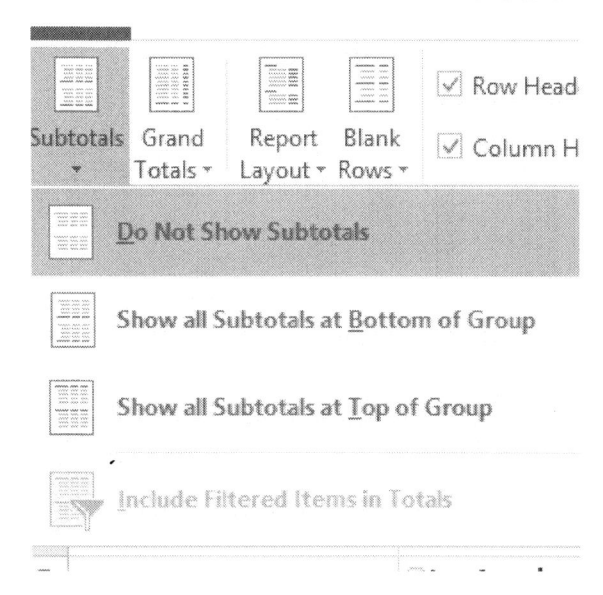

3. Select the desired option.

Sorting

Pivot tables are created already sorted in ascending order (alphabetical or numeric).

The sorting order can be changed by following the steps below:

1. Click on the arrow at the top of the field.

2. Select the desired type of sorting:

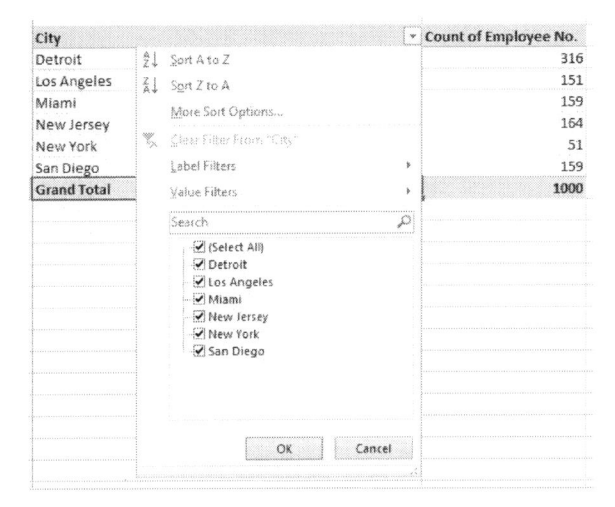

Furthermore, the pivot table enables us to arrange the data by moving the fields to the desired positions:

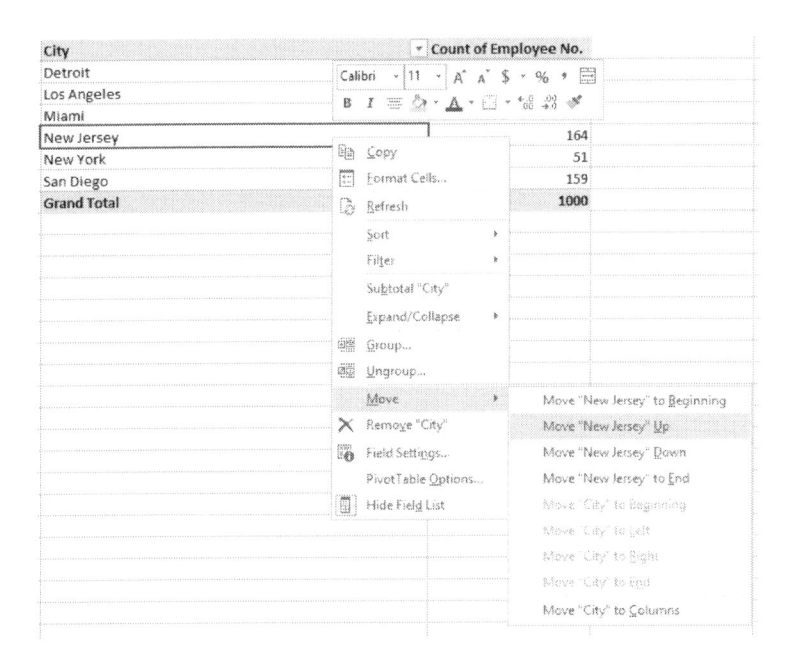

1. Right-click on the item to be repositioned.

2. From the drop-down list, select "**Move**".

3. Choose the new position.

Note that the fields can also be dragged within the pivot table in order to change their location.

Filtering

By default, the pivot table displays all the data fields dragged into it. If we want to view only some of the data, we use the Filter option:

1. Click the arrow at the top of the field.

2. Select the values to be displayed:

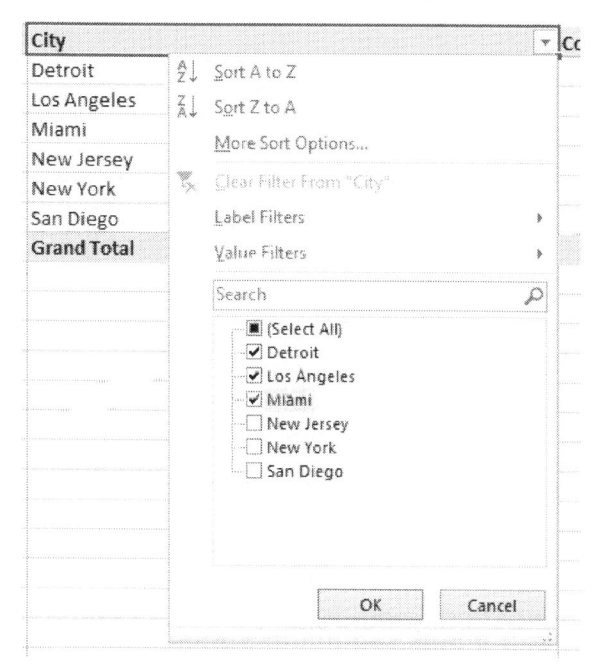

3. Click [OK]

4. The following pivot table will appear:

City	Count of Employee No.
Detroit	316
Los Angeles	151
Miami	159
Grand Total	626

Note that the filter icon has changed from [▼] to [▼filtered], in order to indicate that the data has been filtered.

Removing filtering:

1. Click on the filtering arrow.

2. Select "Clear Filter":

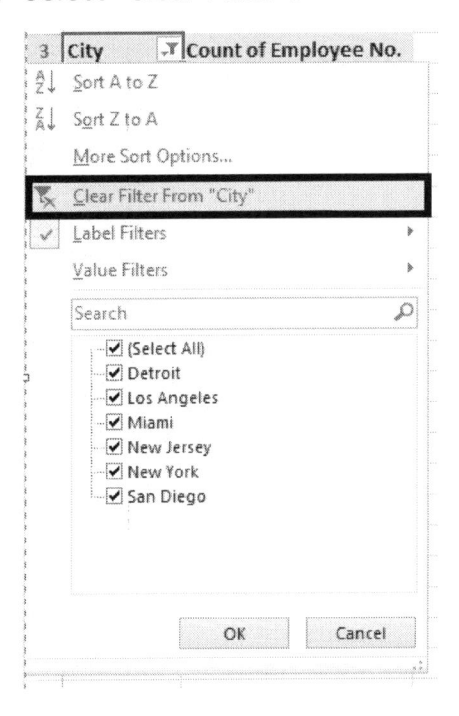

Value Filters:

Pivot tables have other ways to filter data, such as displaying values that are greater than, or less than, a certain value:

1. Click the filtering arrow.
2. Select "**Value Filter**".
3. Select the desired filtering option:

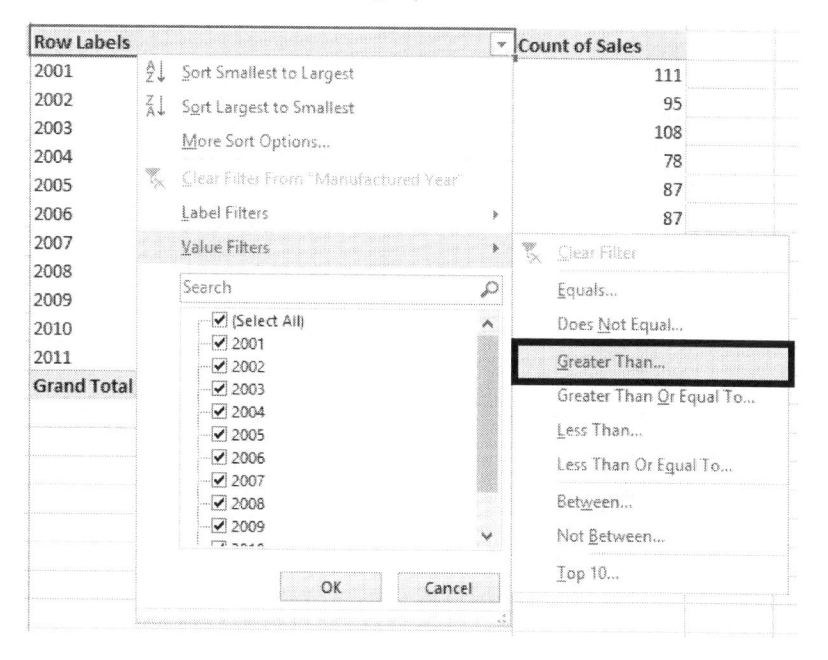

Label Filters:

Excel enables us to filter textual data in many different ways, for example – by displaying textual data that begins with, ends with, contains, or does not contain certain characters.

1. Click on the filtering arrow.

2. Select "**Label Filter**".

3. Select the desired filtering option:

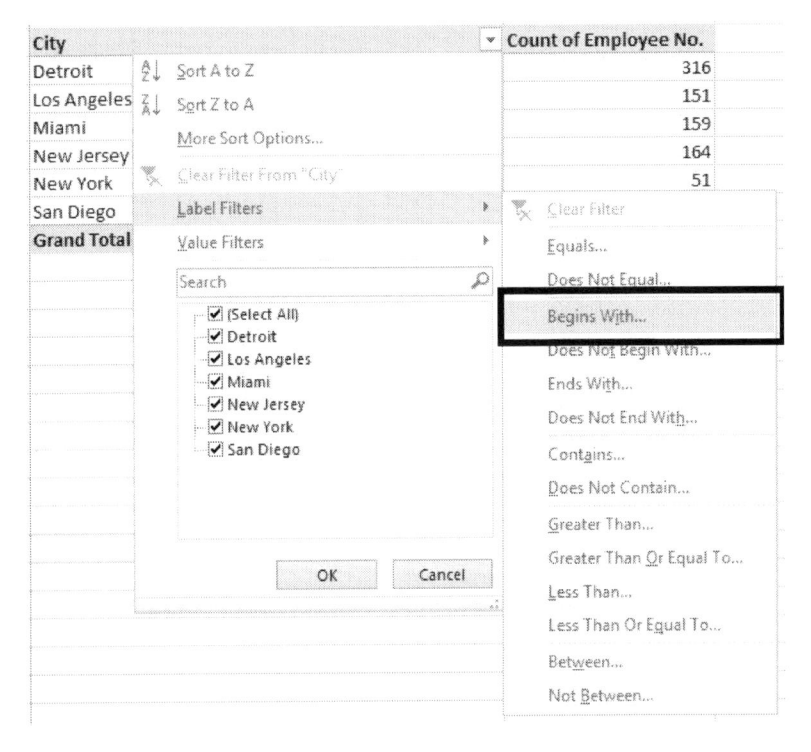

In the following example, we want to see all the city names beginning with the letter N:

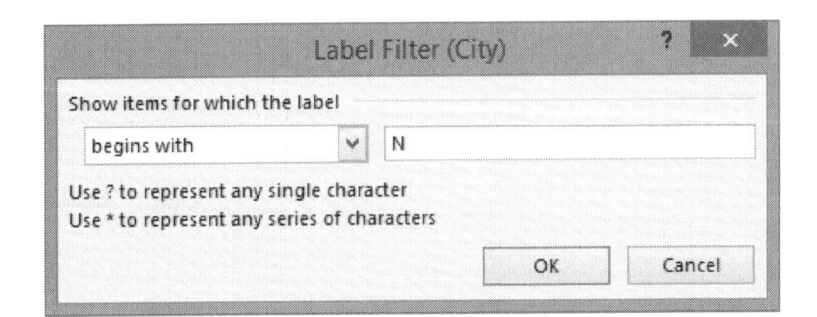

The following pivot table will appear:

City	Count of Employee No.
New Jersey	164
New York	51
Grand Total	215

Removing data which has been deleted from the filter list

Like any database, the tables on which the pivot tables are based, are subject to change. One of the most common changes is the deletion of data.

However, after the data has been deleted, it will still appear in the list of the fields.

To remove deleted data from the filter, follow the next steps:

Select the "**Options**" button under the "**ANALYZE**" tab:

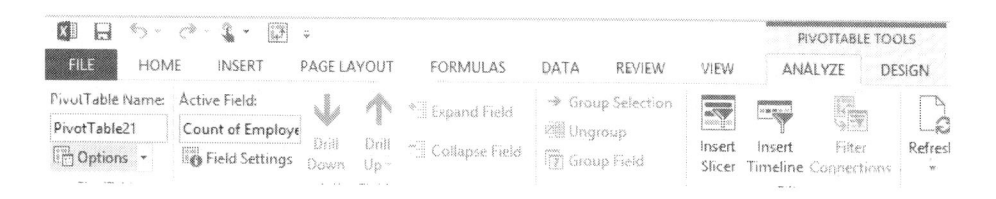

In the following window, Select the "**Data**" tab:

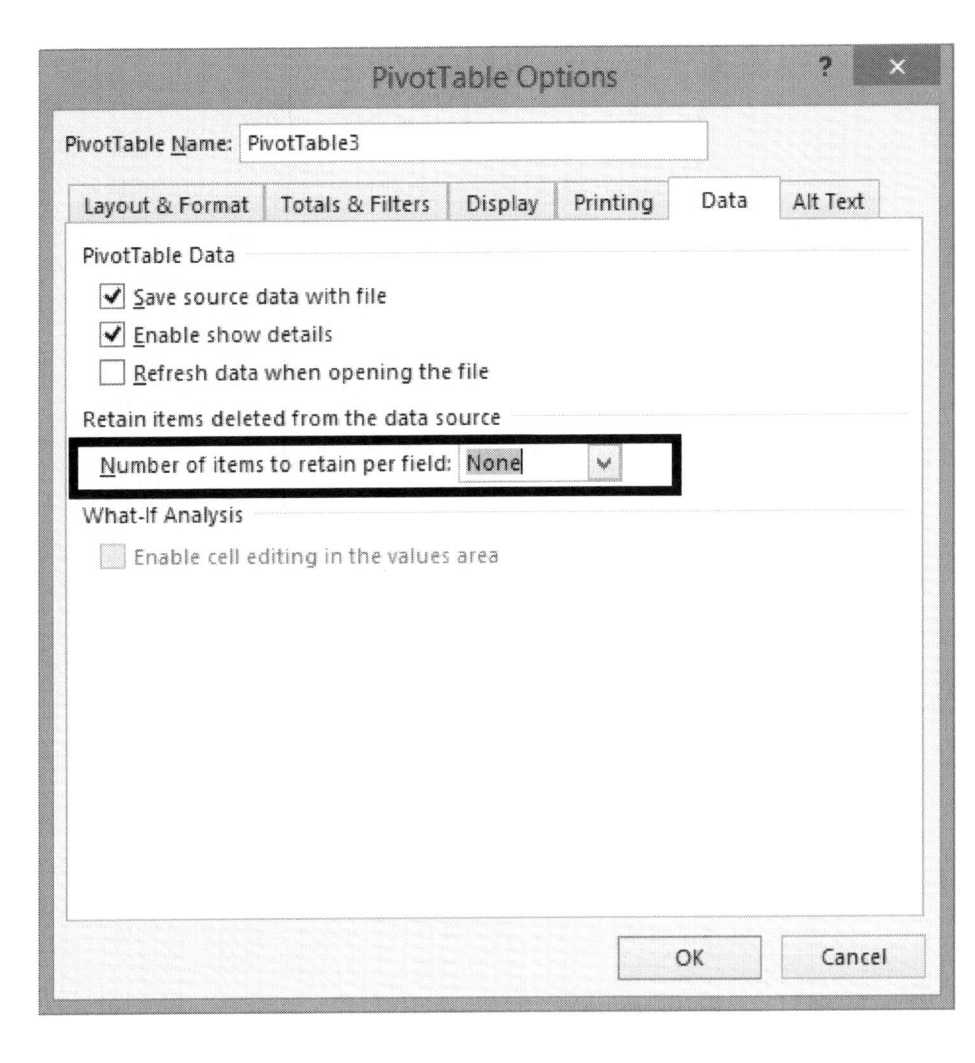

In "**Number of items to retain per field**", select "None".

Slicers

The slicers are a new option that was introduced in the Excel 2010 version. It displays on-screen buttons, enabling us to filter the pivot table data.

This new option is easy to operate, and displays the current filtering state clearly, thus making the report data more readable for the user.

Using the slicers replaces the use of drop-down lists for selecting the items to be filtered (as done with the other filter components).

In order to use the slicers tool, make sure that the file is in the 2010 format at least.

If the file format is an older version, then the slicers option will be disabled and the file will have to be converted to the new version by selecting the **FILE** tab ⟶ **INFO** category ⟶ **CONVERT**.

Note that after the conversion, you will have to close and re-open the worksheet.

After reopening, refresh the pivot tables.

Creating filters using slicers:

Creating the filter

1. Create a pivot table.

2. Under the "**ANALYZE**" tab, select "**Insert Slicers**" (it can also be found in the "**INSERT**" tab):

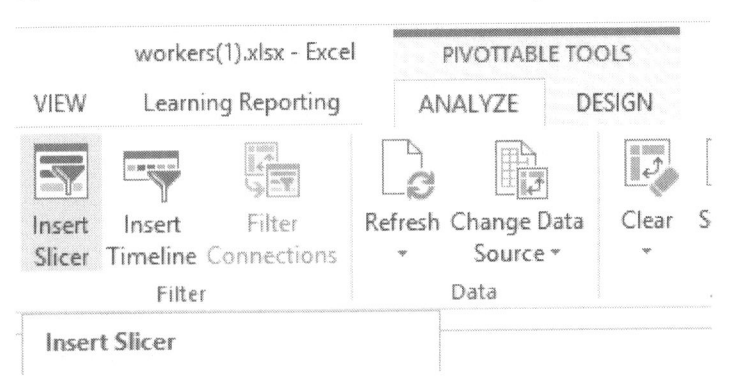

3. The following window will appear:

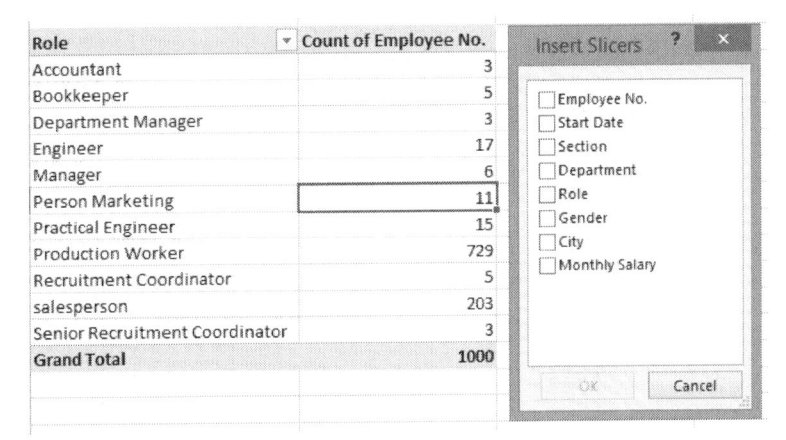

4. Select the fields you want to add as slicers to the pivot table.

5. Click [OK]

6. The following slicer window will appear:

Role	Count of Employee No.
Accountant	3
Bookkeeper	5
Department Manager	3
Engineer	17
Manager	6
Person Marketing	11
Practical Engineer	15
Production Worker	729
Recruitment Coordinator	5
salesperson	203
Senior Recruitment Coordinator	3
Grand Total	**1000**

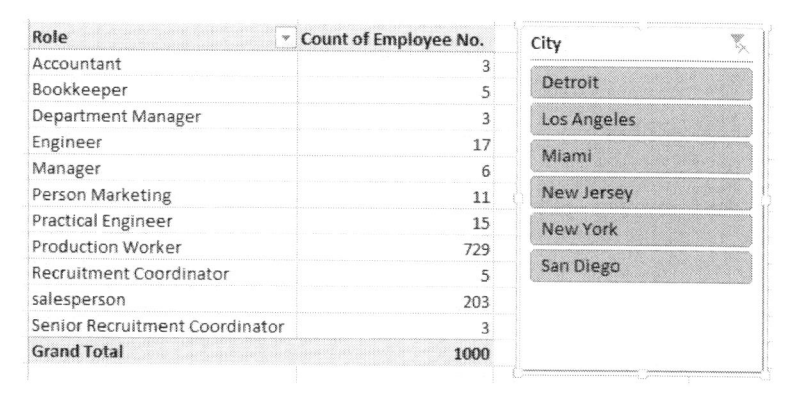

City
- Detroit
- Los Angeles
- Miami
- New Jersey
- New York
- San Diego

7. Once we have selected the items we want, only the filtered records will be displayed:

Role	Count of Employee No.
Engineer	1
Practical Engineer	2
Production Worker	41
Recruitment Coordinator	1
salesperson	6
Grand Total	**51**

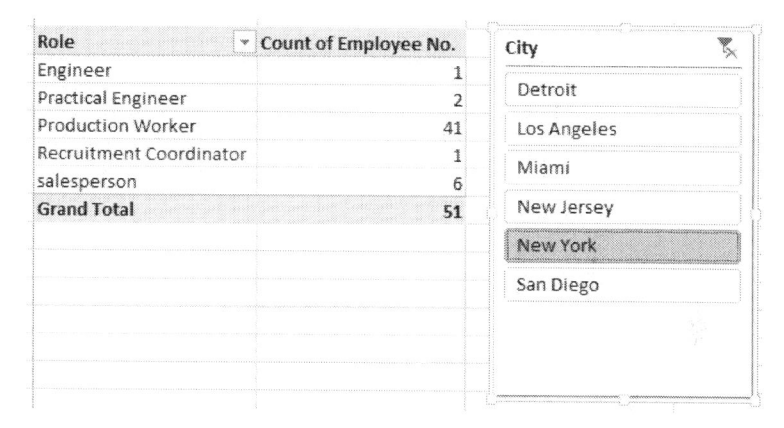

City
- Detroit
- Los Angeles
- Miami
- New Jersey
- **New York**
- San Diego

Note: To select multiple filters, use Ctrl:

Role	Count of Employee No.
Bookkeeper	2
Engineer	5
Person Marketing	1
Practical Engineer	6
Production Worker	154
Recruitment Coordinator	1
salesperson	41
Grand Total	210

City
- Detroit
- Los Angeles
- Miami
- New Jersey
- New York
- San Diego

Manipulating Slicers

1. Select a slicer.

2. The "Slicers" tab will appear.

Changing the slicer's name

1. The caption that will appear as the window title can be changed:

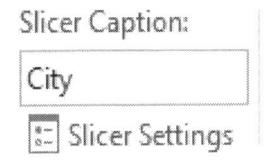

   Slicer Caption:

   City

   Slicer Settings

Creating connections:

If there are a number of pivot tables based on the same data, the slicers can be linked to more than one table:

1. Click [Report Connections]

2. The following window will appear:

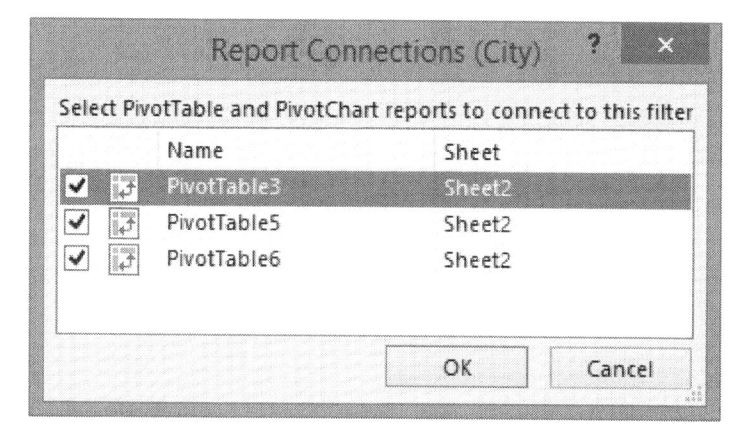

3. Select the desired tables.

Changing the slicer's appearance:

1. Different styles can be selected for the slicers:

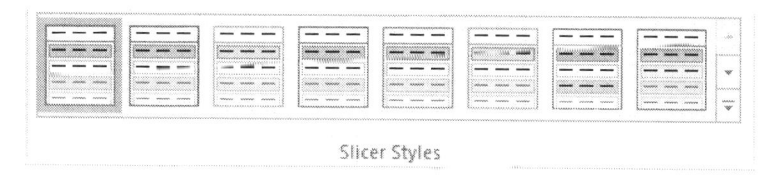

2. The number of columns in the slicer window, and the size of the buttons can be set:

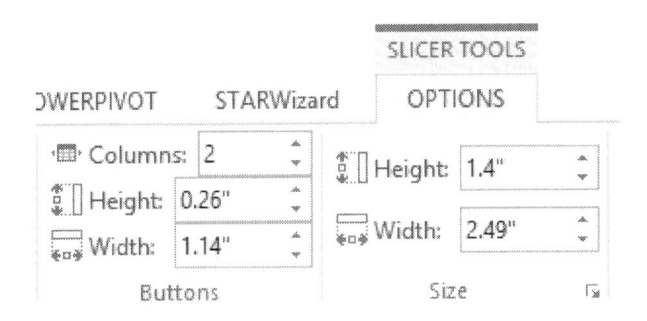

You can see this in the following figure:

Removing items which were deleted from the data source

The slicers can contain items which were deleted from the data source after they were created.

These items can be removed as follows:

1. Select the Slicers window.

2. Under " **SLICER TOOLS** " → "**OPTIONS**" tab, click Slicer Settings

3. The following window will appear:

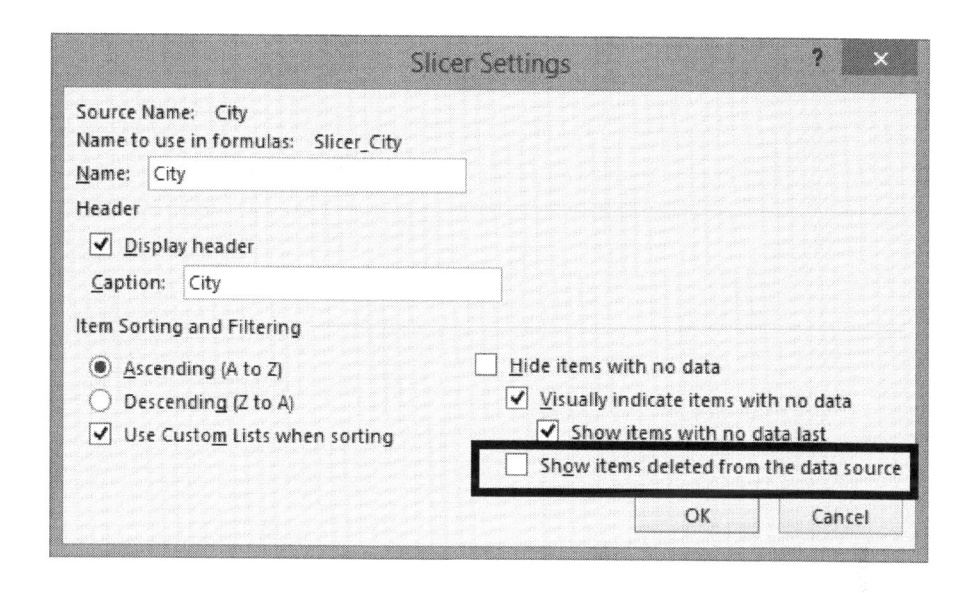

4. Uncheck "**Show items deleted from the data source**".

The Timeline

Another tool that enables us to filter the data is the Timeline, which helps us filter the records by dates.

Insert Timeline:

1. Create a pivot table.

2. Under the "**ANALYZE**" tab, select "**Insert Timeline**":

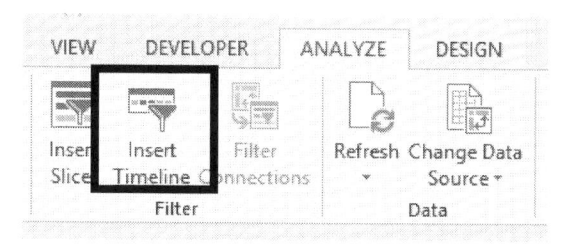

3. A window that contains date fields will appear:

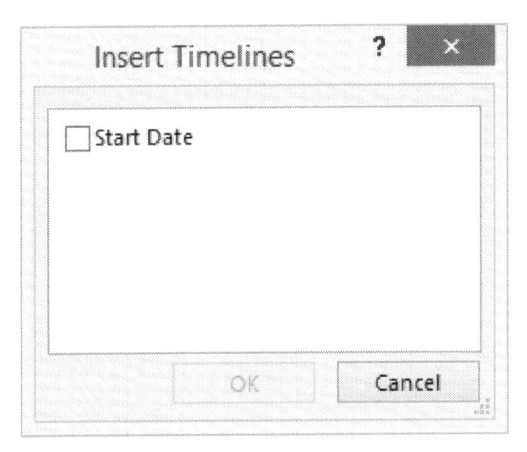

4. Select the desired field.

5. Click [OK]

6. The timeline will appear:

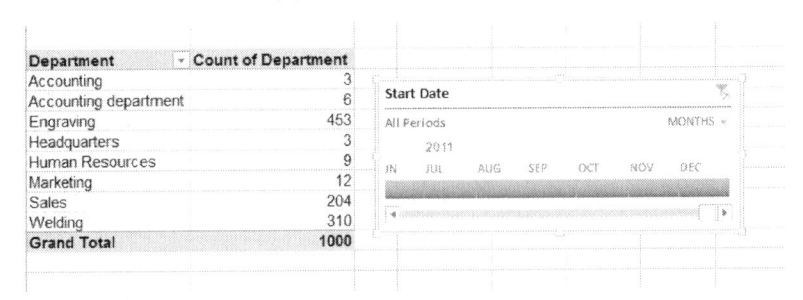

7. Choose the desired period by selecting it on the Timeline:

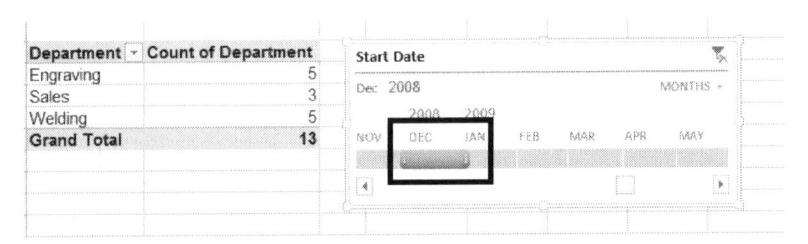

In order to select a continuous period, simply drag the cursor over it:

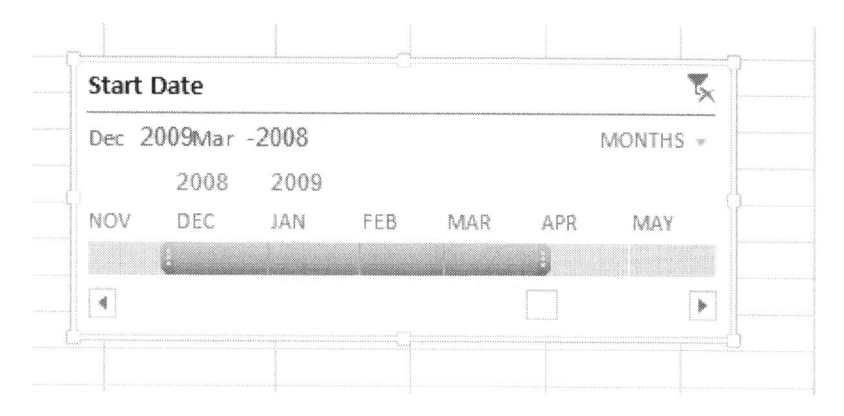

Changing the time period:

1. Click on the arrow, as shown in the following image:

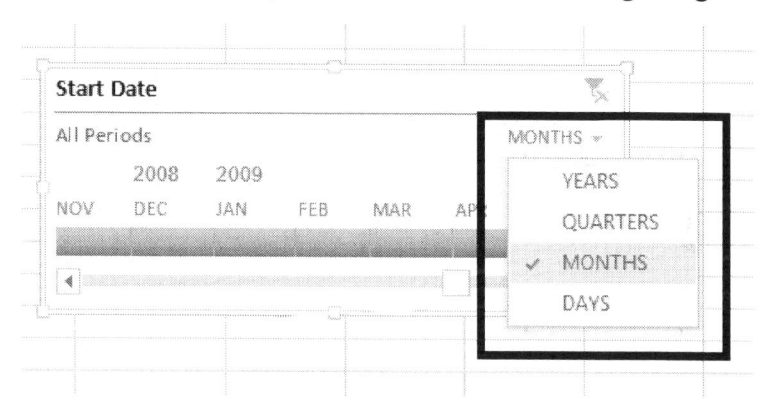

2. Select the desired time period.

Changing the Timeline's appearance:

Different styles can be selected for the Timeline:

- Select the "**OPTIONS**" tab under the "**TIMELINE TOOLS**" tab:

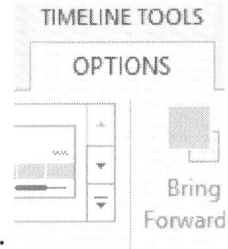

- Change the Timeline caption:

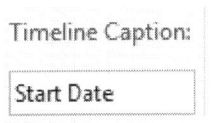

- Select a style:

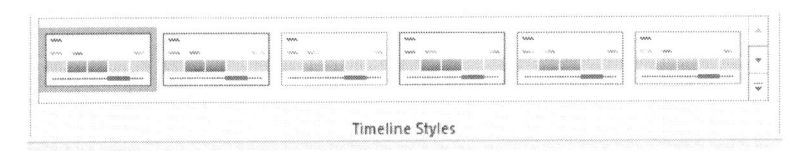

- Select the Timeline size:

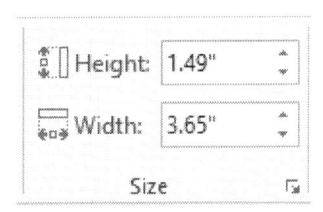

(You can also change the size of the Timeline by dragging its borders.)

- Show or hide the Headers, Selection Label and Time Level, or the appearance of the scroll bar:

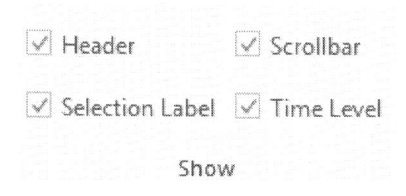

  ☑ Header ☑ Scrollbar
  ☑ Selection Label ☑ Time Level
  Show

- Connect it to numerous pivot tables by pressing the Report Connections button, and selecting the desired pivot tables.

Exercises

1. Display the desired average sale price by: engine capacity, year of manufacture and type of gear. Paint the subtotals in yellow.

2. Cancel the subtotals from the previous report.

3. Display the desired price average by date of sale. Sort the table in descending order, by date.

4. Display the average sale price by color.

5. Move the white-colored cars to the bottom of the table.

6. Display the number of cars by country of manufacture. Using a filter, display European cars only.

7. Display the number of cars by make. Using a filter, display the car names starting with "S" only.

8. Create a pivot table report in which the make will appear in the ROWS and the average desired price will appear in the VALUES. Display the country of manufacture using slicers.

Design Tab

Pivot tables can be formatted by using the cell formatting options, and also by various other tools.

Formatting commands can be found in the "**PIVOTTABLE TOOLS**" → "**DESIGN**" tab and are divided into different categories:

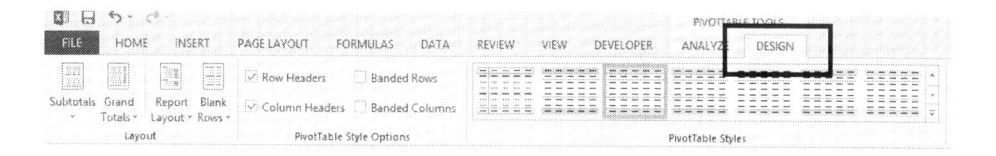

Layout category

- **Subtotals** - this enables us to cancel subtotals, or to show them above or below the group.
- **Totals** - this enables us to show or hide the totals in ROWS and COLUMNS.
- **Report layout** - this enables us to view the pivot table in a compact, outline or tabular form. We can also use it to repeat or cancel the repetition of labels.
- **Blank rows** - this enables us to create or remove blank rows between items.

Pivot table style options

- **Row Headers** - this enables us to display or cancel the bolding of items.
- **Column Headers** - this enables us to display or cancel the bolding of fields.
- **Banded Row/ Banded Column** – this paints the rows or columns alternately.

Quick design styles of pivot table

This enables us to choose between different styles, as shown in the tab.

Choosing a new style

To create a new design for the pivot table:

1. Click "**New Pivot Table Style**":

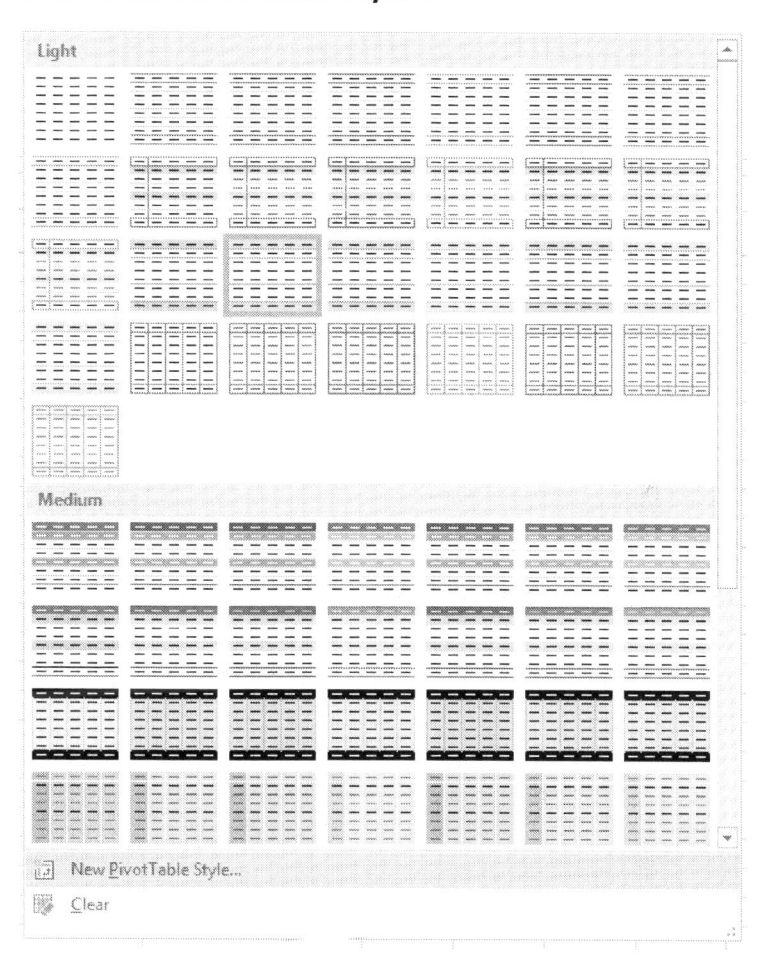

2. The following window will appear:

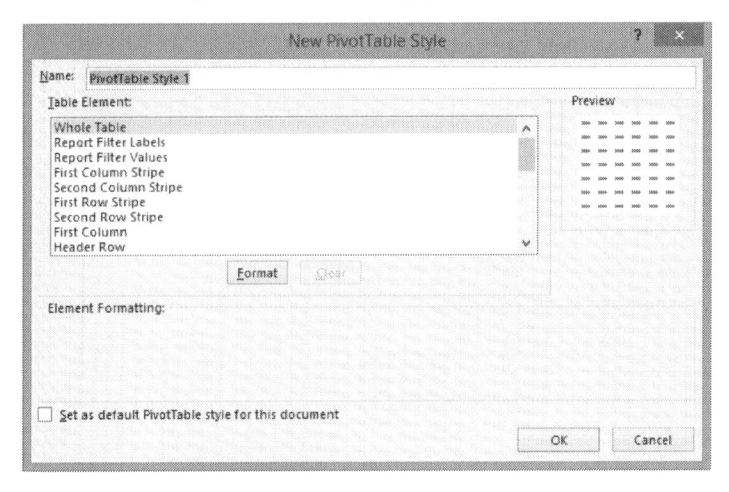

3. Name the newly defined style and design the table components as desired.

4. The new style will appear at the top of the customization list, in the gallery.

Exercises

1. Display the average sale price, divided by make, color and country of manufacture.

2. Cancel the subtotals and the grand total.

3. Switch the report layout to a tabular form.

Charts

So far, we have learned how to create pivot tables to display data in different intersections. Excel also enables us to create charts based on the pivot table, for a more visual display of the data. A chart can be added to an existing pivot table, or created at the same time as a pivot table.

Adding a chart to an existing pivot table

1. Place the cursor in the pivot table.
2. Select the "**ANALYZE**" tab ⟶ "**PivotChart**":

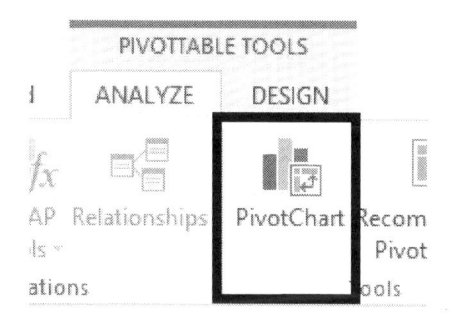

3. The following window will appear:

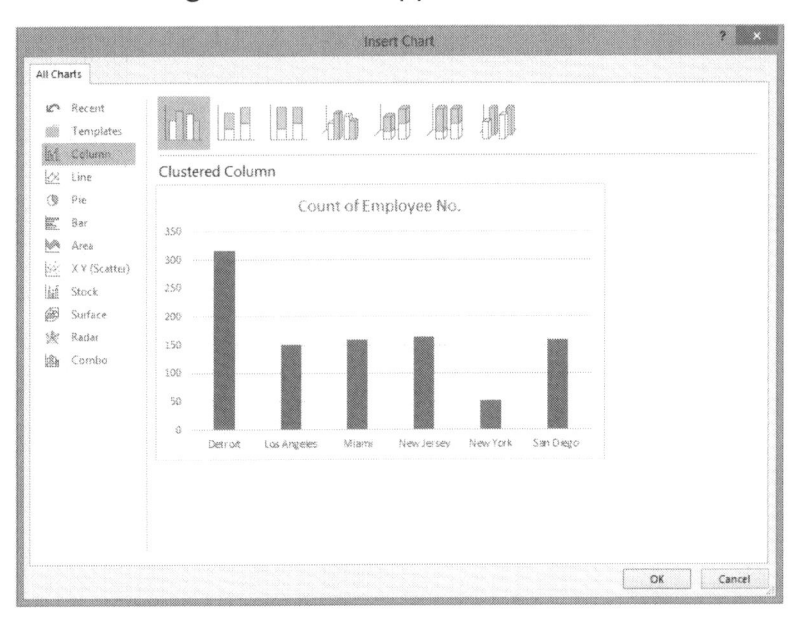

4. Select the desired chart type.

5. Click [OK]

6. The selected chart will appear:

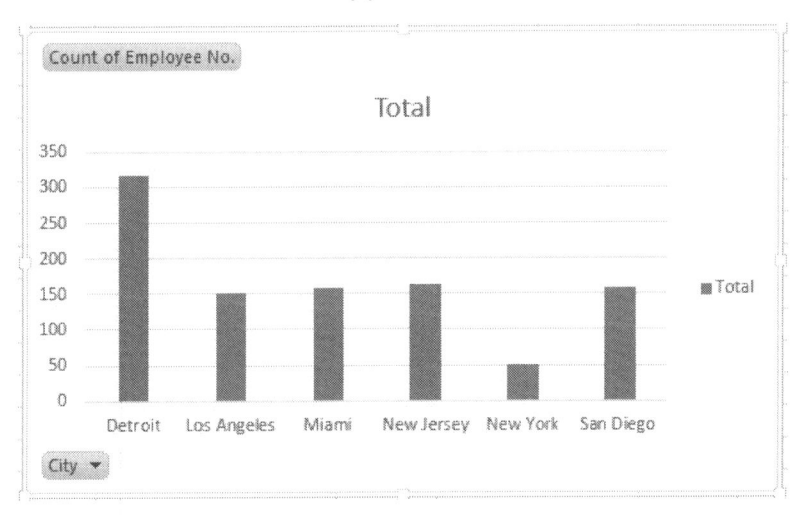

Note: You can also create a chart based on the pivot table, using the "INSERT" tab to select the desired chart type.

Simultaneously creating a pivot table and a chart

- Place the cursor on the data table.
- Select the "INSERT" tab.
- Click the arrow below the PivotChart button.
- Select "**PivotChart & PivotTable**":

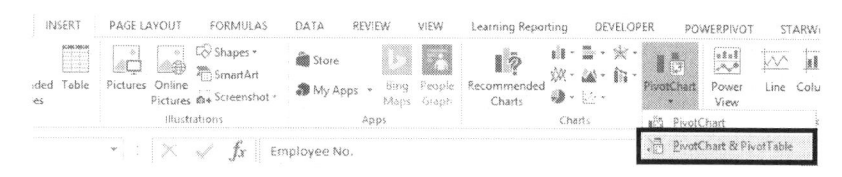

- The pivot table and the pivot chart will appear in the same window:

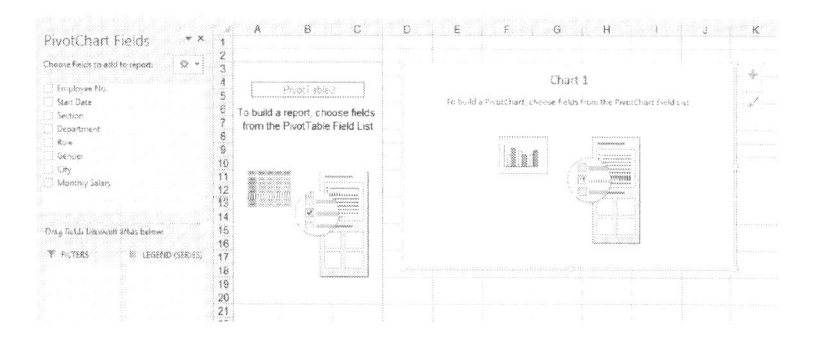

- Dragging the fields to the desired areas will display them in the PivotTable and the PivotChart simultaneously.

Exercises

1. Display the average sale price by make and color.

2. Create a chart based on the pivot table you created.

Tips and Tricks

Using Recommended PivotTables

Excel 2013 has the ability to analyze the data, and recommend the most suitable pivot tables for it.

To use this feature, locate the cursor in a cell in your data table, and under the "INSERT" tab, click Recommended PivotTables

Excel will suggest a list of pivot tables:

Select the one that suits your needs.

Quickly creating a pivot table

A pivot table can be created quickly by copying an existing pivot table, pasting and customizing it, according to your needs.

Obtaining the data source

A pivot table is created from raw data to display grouped data.

The reverse action can be performed as well: displaying the constituting records of an item in the pivot table (Drill down).

In this example, the pivot table displays the number of employees in each role:

Role	Count of Employee No.
Accountant	3
Bookkeeper	5
Department Manager	3
Engineer	17
Manager	6
Person Marketing	11
Practical Engineer	15
Production Worker	729
Recruitment Coordinator	5
Salesperson	203
Senior Recruitment Coordinator	3
Grand Total	**1000**

In order to see the original records, double-click the desired value. In the example above, double-clicking on the number 3 next to "Accountant" will display a new worksheet containing the records which created the result 3.

Employee No.	Start Date	Section	Department	Role	Gender	City	Monthly Salary
W1317	04-05-06	Manageme	Accounting	Accountan	Female	Detroit	4841
W1316	08-03-08	Manageme	Accounting	Accountan	Male	Detroit	4527
W1315	08-12-10	Manageme	Accounting	Accountan	Female	Detroit	4285

Creating Tabs from Filters

A pivot table enables us to split the primary pivot table data into tabs, by using the filtering field.

For example, from a pivot table counting the number of employees in each role, we can create a tab for each section, as explained below:

1. Create a pivot table.

2. Drag the relevant field into the FILTER, as shown in the following figure:

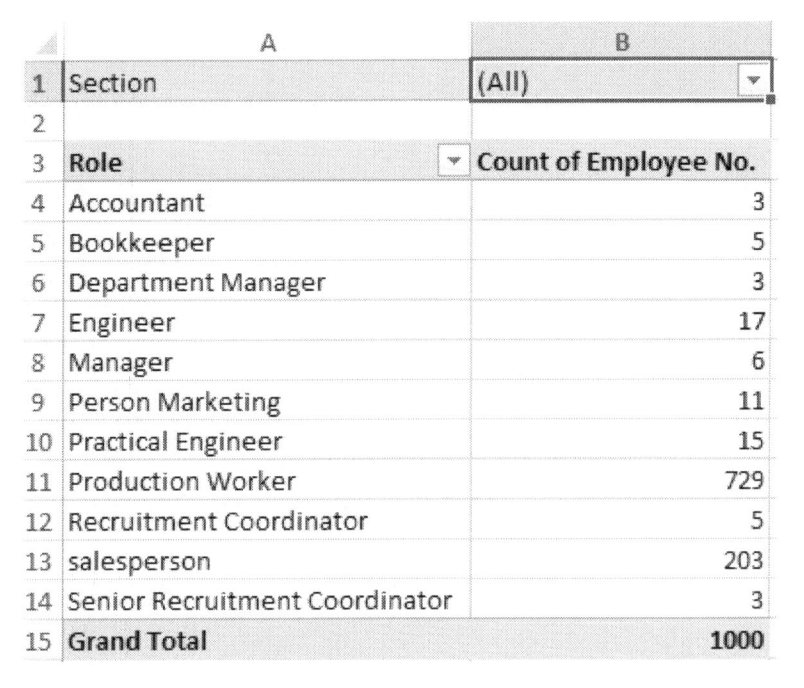

	A	B
1	Section	(All)
2		
3	Role	Count of Employee No.
4	Accountant	3
5	Bookkeeper	5
6	Department Manager	3
7	Engineer	17
8	Manager	6
9	Person Marketing	11
10	Practical Engineer	15
11	Production Worker	729
12	Recruitment Coordinator	5
13	salesperson	203
14	Senior Recruitment Coordinator	3
15	Grand Total	1000

3. Select the "**ANALYZE**" tab ⟶ "**Options**" button.

4. Select "**Show Report Filter Pages**":

5. The following window will appear:

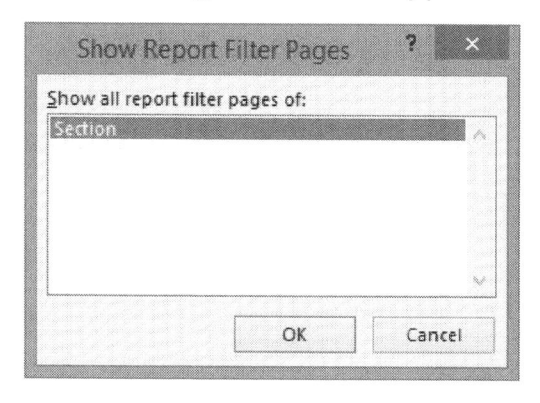

   Show Report Filter Pages

   Show all report filter pages of:

   Section

   OK   Cancel

6. Select the filter with the data to be displayed in the tabs and click OK

Now the file contains tabs by the names of items dragged to the FILTER. Each of the tabs consists only of the relevant data:

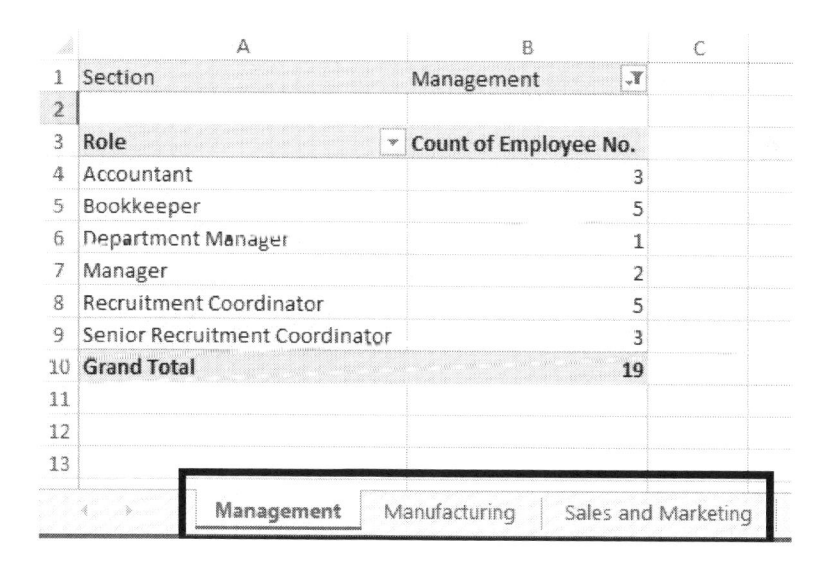

	A	B	C
1	Section	Management	
2			
3	Role	Count of Employee No.	
4	Accountant	3	
5	Bookkeeper	5	
6	Department Manager	1	
7	Manager	2	
8	Recruitment Coordinator	5	
9	Senior Recruitment Coordinator	3	
10	Grand Total	19	
11			
12			
13			

Management | Manufacturing | Sales and Marketing

123

Filter Locations

By default, the page filters are displayed in one column, as shown in the following example:

Section	(All)
Department	(All)
Gender	(All)
City	(All)

Role	Count of Employee No.
Accountant	3
Bookkeeper	5
Department Manager	3
Engineer	17
Manager	6
Person Marketing	11
Practical Engineer	15
Production Worker	729
Recruitment Coordinator	5
salesperson	203
Senior Recruitment Coordinator	3
Grand Total	1000

Excel enables us to separate the filters into several columns, by following the steps below:

1. Click the "**ANALYZE**" Tab.

2. Click "**Options**":

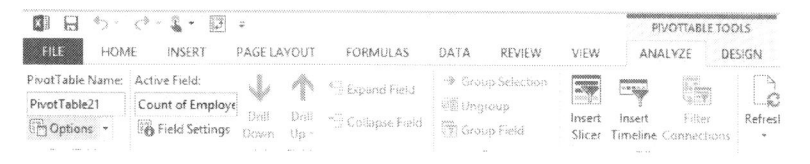

3. The following window will appear:

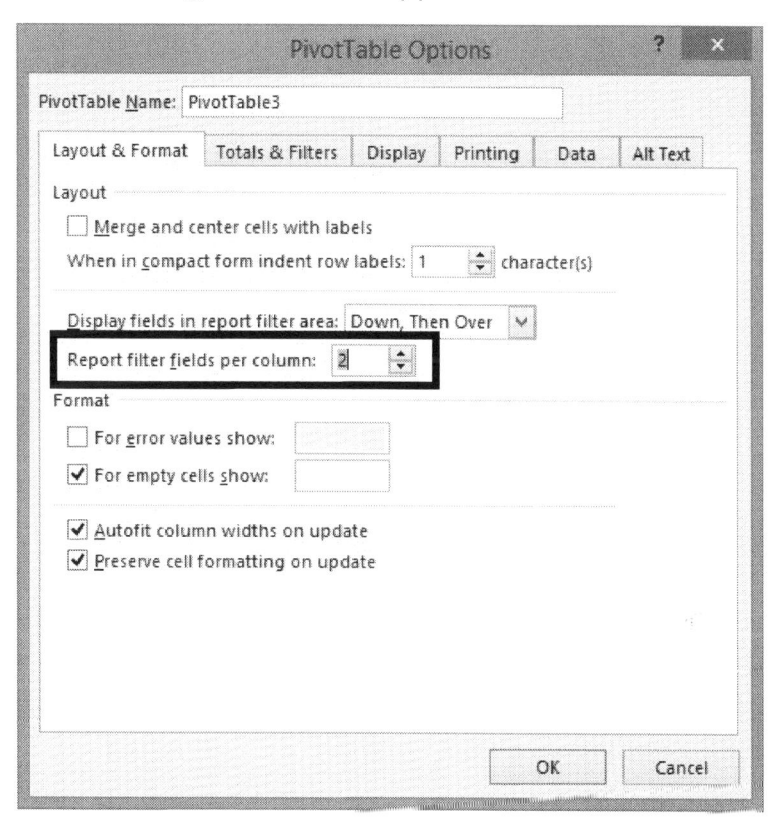

4. In the "**Layout & Format**" tab, change "**Report filter fields per column**" to the desired value.

5. The filters in the resulting pivot table are now divided into columns:

Section	(All)		Gender	(All)
Department	(All)		City	(All)

Role	Count of Employee No.
Accountant	3
Bookkeeper	5
Department Manager	3
Engineer	17
Manager	6
Person Marketing	11
Practical Engineer	15
Production Worker	729
Recruitment Coordinator	5
salesperson	203
Senior Recruitment Coordinator	3
Grand Total	1000

GetPivotData

The GetPivotData function is designed to find the intersected value between fields (i.e, City and Gender).

Whenever we use data from a pivot table in our Excel formulas, the function is created automatically.

However, since the default of the GetPivotData function is an absolute reference (as opposed to Excel's functions, where the default is a relative reference), you may want to cancel the GetPivotData function when applying it to the pivot tables.

To cancel this feature:

1. Select "**PIVOTTABLE TOOLS**" →"**ANALYZE**" tab → "**Options**" button.

2. Uncheck "**Generate GetPivotData**".

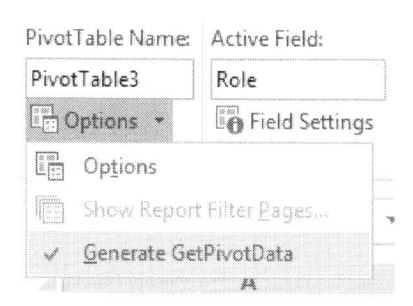

If you prefer to keep the GetPivotData function, you can use a relative reference by typing the reference to the cell (instead of pointing at the cell with the cursor).

Sorting the field list

When creating a pivot table, the Field List appears in the same order as in the data table:

127

We can sort the field list alphabetically, as follows:

1. Select the "**ANALYZE**" tab ⟶ "**Options**" button.

2. In the "**Display**" Tab, select "**Sort A to Z**":

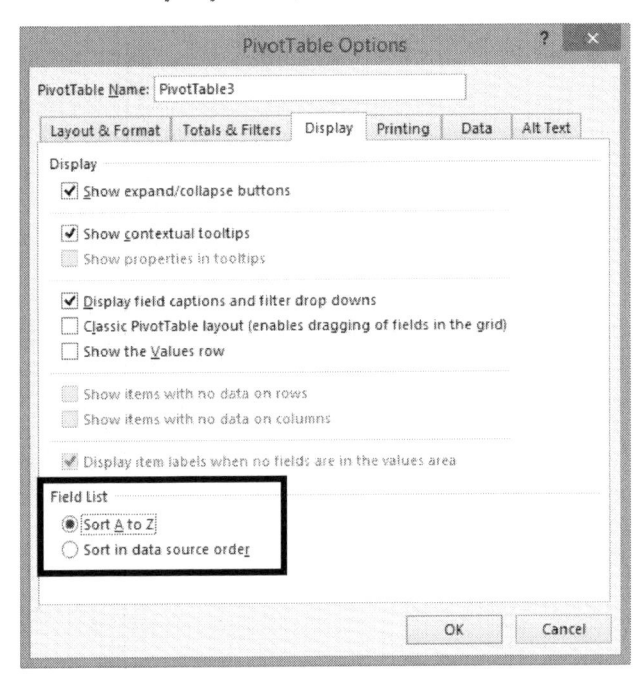

3. The field list will be sorted accordingly:

Repeating the item labels

We have created a pivot table that counts the number of employees, divided into department and section, and formatted it as a table:

Section	Department	Count of Employee No.
⊟ Management	Accounting	3
	accounting department	6
	headquarters	1
	Human Resources	9
Management Total		19
⊟ Manufacturing	Engraving	453
	headquarters	1
	Welding	310
Manufacturing Total		764
⊟ Sales and Marketing	headquarters	1
	Marketing	12
	Sales	204
Sales and Marketing Total		217
Grand Total		1000

Although this pivot table is readable for the user, it makes it difficult for Excel to perform calculations designed to retrieve information from it (e.g. INDEX, MATCH).

To normalize the table, follow the steps below:

1. Place the cursor inside the pivot table.

2. Under "**PIVOTTABLE TOOLS**", select the "**DESIGN**" tab:

3. Under "**Report Layout**", select "**Repeat All Item Labels**":

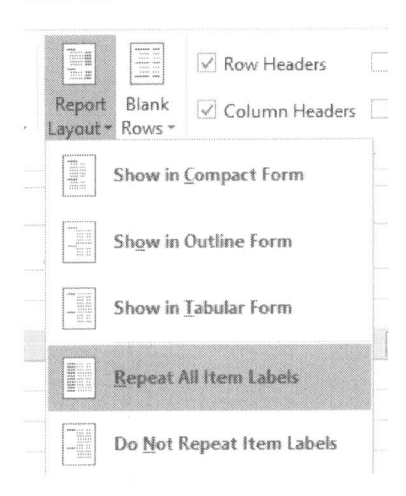

4. The following pivot table will appear:

Section	Department	Count of Employee No.
⊟ Management	Accounting	3
Management	Accounting department	6
Management	Headquarters	1
Management	Human Resources	9
Management Total		**19**
⊟ Manufacturing	Engraving	453
Manufacturing	Headquarters	1
Manufacturing	Welding	310
Manufacturing Total		**764**
⊟ Sales and Marketing	Headquarters	1
Sales and Marketing	Marketing	12
Sales and Marketing	Sales	204
Sales and Marketing Total		**217**
Grand Total		**1000**

Now we can use the table as a source of desired calculations.

Advanced Uses of Pivot Tables

Finding unique records and duplicate records

A pivot table enables us to find duplicate records in a database.

In this example, we have obtained lists of registered members of two political parties, and we want to check if there are people who are illegally registered to both parties, and which people are registered to only one party.

ID	Party
4130	A
2807	A
1650	A
4876	A
3438	A
3116	A
4554	A
2418	A
1213	A
3940	A
3068	B
4537	B
1650	B
2922	B
4294	B
3335	B
4554	B
4111	B
3827	B
4130	B
4732	B

We have created a pivot table in which we dragged the ID records to the ROWS and the party registration field to the COLUMNS. We also dragged the ID field to the VALUES:

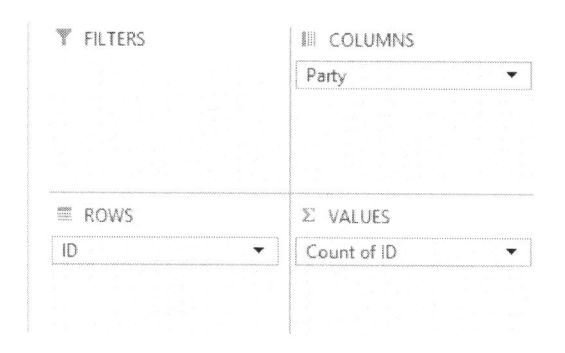

```
▼ FILTERS                III COLUMNS
                         Party          ▼


≡ ROWS                   Σ VALUES
ID              ▼        Count of ID    ▼
```

The following pivot table appears:

Count of ID	Party		
ID	A	B	Grand Total
1213	1		1
1650	1	1	2
2110	1		1
2807	1		1
2922		1	1
3068		1	1
3116	1		1
3335		1	1
3438	1		1
3827		1	1
3940	1		1
4111		1	1
4130	1	1	2
4294		1	1
4537		1	1
4554	1	1	2
4732		1	1
4876	1		1
Grand Total	10	11	21

From the pivot table above, it appears that the owner of ID 1650 was registered to both parties A and B, while the owner of ID 1213 was registered to party A only.

Human Resources Planning

The director of the Human Resources Department conducts an annual staffing plan. He is provided with departmental requests about specific needs, moves people from one department to another, outsources and fires employees, etc.

The raw data is shown in the following table:

From	To	No. of Employees
Purchase	sales	10
Purchase	HR	15
sales	Purchase	20
sales	HR	25
HR	Purchase	30
HR	sales	35
Purchase	Retired	40
sales	Fired	45
HR	Resign	50
Recruitment	Purchase	55
Recruitment	sales	60
Recruitment	HR	65

As shown in the data table, 10 employees are to be transferred from the Purchase Department to the Sales Department, and 15 employees are to be transferred from the Purchase Department to the Human Resources Department.

In order to know more about the transfers between departments, we can create a pivot table, where the source will appear in rows and the target will appear in columns. The number of employees will be represented in the values:

Sum of No. of Employees	Column Labels						
Row Labels	Fired	HR	Purchase	Resign	Retired	sales	Grand Total
HR			30	50		35	115
Purchase		15			40	10	65
Recruitment		65	55			60	180
sales	45	25	20				90
Grand Total	45	105	105	50	40	105	450

Now it is easier to review the transfers of employees to and from different departments.

For example, it is easy to see that 25 employees moved from the Sales Department to the Human Resources department, 20 employees moved from the Sales Department to the Purchase Department and 45 employees were fired from the Sales Department.

We can also see that 60 employees were recruited for the Sales Department, 65 employees were recruited for the Human Resources department and 55 were recruited for the Purchase Department.

From the total row, we learn that 105 employees moved to the Sales Department and 90 are no longer employed at the factory.

Cash Flow

A business owner enters his customers' payment data into the Excel table below:

Customer	Pay Date	Expected Pay	Actual Pay
Dan	3/1/2014	$ 1,000	$ 1,000
Dan	4/1/2014	$ 1,000	$ 900
Dan	5/1/2014	$ 2,000	
Dan	6/1/2014	$ 6,000	
John	4/1/2014	$ 1,000	$ 1,000
John	5/1/2014	$ 1,000	$ 900
John	6/1/2014	$ 1,000	
John	7/1/2014	$ 2,000	
Amy	3/1/2014	$ 1,000	$ 1,000
Amy	4/1/2014	$ 1,000	$ 900
Amy	5/1/2014	$ 2,000	
Amy	6/1/2014	$ 6,000	

The table displays the customer's name, date of payment, expected payment, and the actual payment. The cash flow can be derived from the data table by dragging the date of payment to the ROWS and the expected payment to the VALUES:

Row Labels	Sum of Expected Pay
3/1/2014	2000
4/1/2014	3000
5/1/2014	5000
6/1/2014	13000
7/1/2014	2000
Grand Total	25000

From the pivot table we can conclude that on 3/1/2014, a sum of 2,000 USD is expected to be deposited in the business account.

The same data table can be used to view the status of customer payments, with details of the expected payment and the actual payment.

The balance due was calculated using "Calculated Field" (see page 65)

Row Labels	Sum of Expected Pay	Sum of Balance Due
3/1/2014	2000	0
4/1/2014	3000	200
5/1/2014	5000	4100
6/1/2014	13000	13000
7/1/2014	2000	2000
Grand Total	25000	19300

Profit and Loss

A factory manager enters the factory revenue and expenses to the following table:

Expense	Detail	Amount
Sales Income	Shirts	$ 500,000.00
Sales Income	trousers	$ 750,000.00
Sales Income	skirts	$ 80,000.00
Sales Income	belts	$ 50,000.00
Sales Income	shoes	$ 800,000.00
Expenses	workers	$ 50,000.00
Expenses	niddles	$ 120,000.00
Expenses	fabrics	$ 130,000.00
Expenses	buttons	$ 140,000.00
Management	Senior Man	$ 5,000.00
Management	Mangers	$ 6,000.00
Management	Section Em	$ 7,000.00
Management	other	$ 8,000.00
Taxes	IRS	$ 1,000.00
Taxes	Social Secu	$ 1,100.00

In order to create a profit and loss statement, we have to create the following pivot table:

Row Labels	Sum of Amount
Expenses	440000
Management	26000
Sales Income	2180000
Taxes	2100
Grand Total	2648100

In order to view the Profit & Loss Statement, we have to re-order the data by dragging the revenue data from sales and placing it before the expenses data:

Row Labels	Sum of Amount
Sales Income	2180000
Expenses	440000
Management	26000
Taxes	2100
Grand Total	**2648100**

We can now use "Calculated Item" in order to perform the calculations of gross profit, operating profit, and net profit:

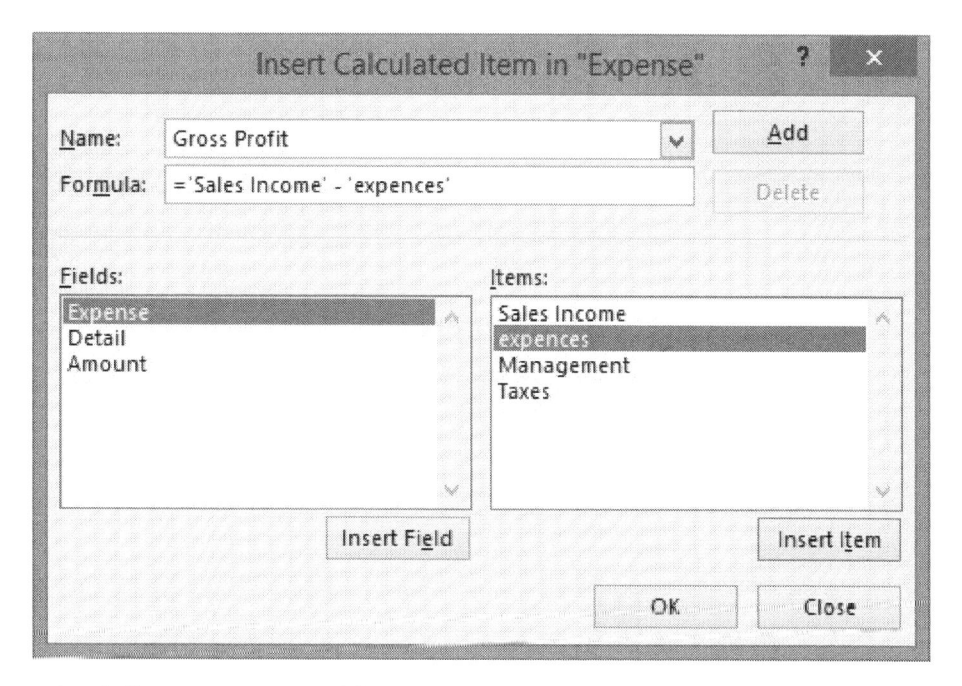

The following pivot table appears:

Row Labels	Sum of Amount
Sales Income	2180000
expences	440000
Management	26000
Taxes	2100
Gross Profit	1740000
Operating Profit	1714000
Net Profit	1711900
Grand Total	7814000

Now all we have to do is to move the calculated items to the appropriate position:

Row Labels	Sum of Amount
Sales Income	2180000
expences	440000
Gross Profit	**1740000**
Management	26000
Operating Profit	**1714000**
Taxes	2100
Net Profit	**1711900**
Grand Total	7814000

The pivot table above shows the factory's Profit & Loss Statement.

Note that the bold columns are the result of a calculated item from data in the original pivot table.

Appendix

Selecting data from other file types

You may sometimes need to create pivot tables using data from other file types, such as Microsoft Access, SQL database, etc.

In order to create the data table, we first need to connect to the database as follows:

1. In the "INS **Headers** ERT" tab, select "**PivotTable**".
2. The following window will appear:

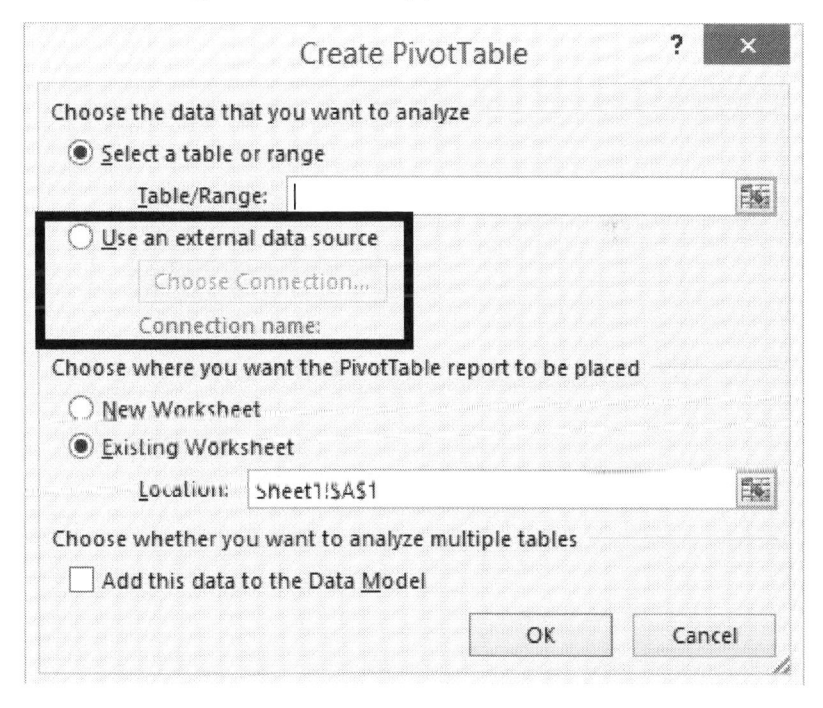

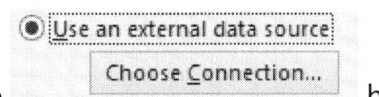

3. Click the **Use an external data source / Choose Connection...** button.

4. The "**Existing Connections**" window will appear:

Note: The window may look different on your computer, depending on the current connections.

5. Click **Browse for More...**

6. The "**Select Data Source**" window will appear:

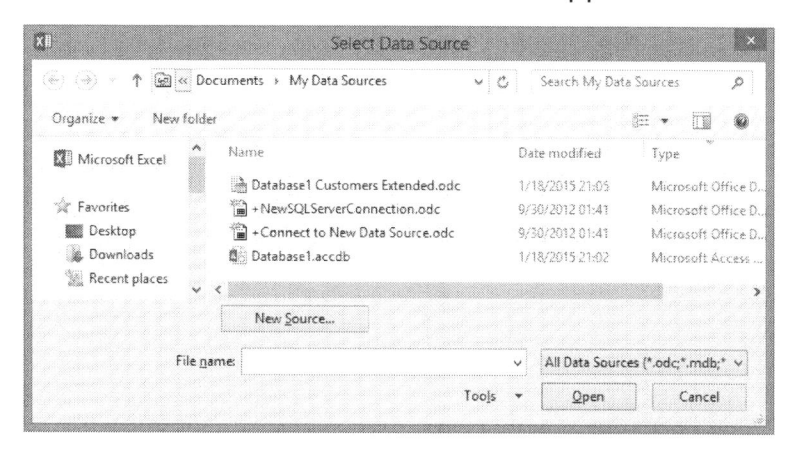

7. Navigate to the folder where the data file is located and select the file.

8. Click [Open]

9. In the following example we selected an Access database.

10. The "**Select Table**" window will appear:

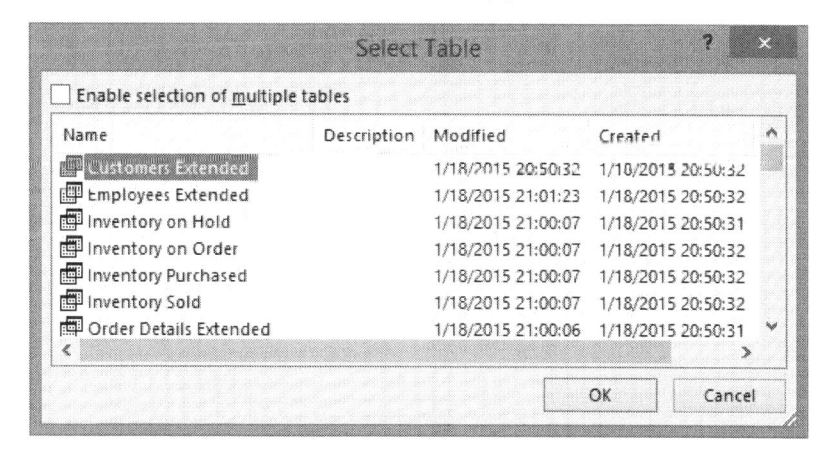

143

11. Select the relevant table.

12. Click [OK]

13. An empty pivot table that contains the fields of the selected table will appear.

Pivot Tables Wizard

In older versions of Excel, users could build the pivot table step by step, using the Pivot Tables Wizard.

The wizard included other options as well, such as "multiple consolidation ranges", which do not appear in the Ribbon Versions (Excel 2007 and higher).

Users who are accustomed to using the wizard, or using the options available, can add it to the Quick Access Toolbar:

1. Click the arrow in the Quick Access Toolbar.

2. Select "**More Commands**":

3. The following window will appear:

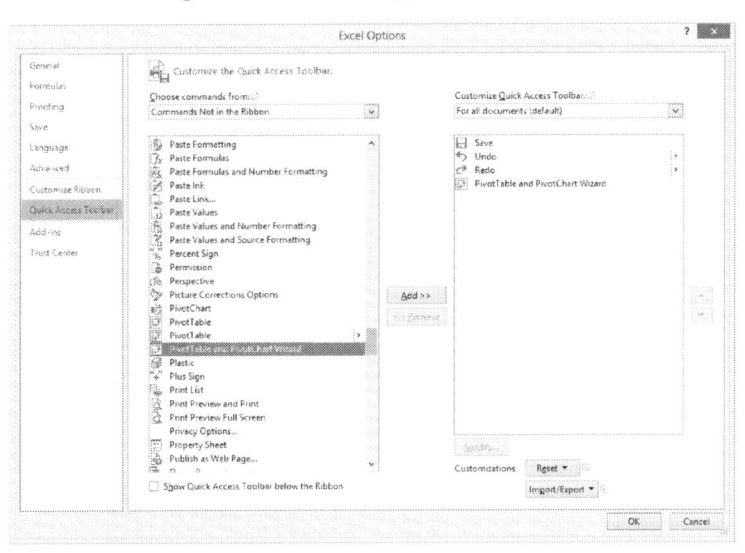

4. From "**Commands Not in the Ribbon**", select "**PivotTable and PivotChart Wizard**".

5. Click [Add >>]

6. Click [OK]

7. The Pivot Tables Wizard will be added to the Quick Access Toolbar:

Multiple Consolidation Ranges

You might sometimes need to create a PivotTable report based on different tables.

It is recommended to unite the tables into a single table.

However, Excel allows us to create pivot tables that are based on Multiple Consolidation Ranges, that is - on a number of tables that contain data in the same structure.

Before creating a table, make sure that the titles in the tables are all identical.

In the following example, we have an Excel file that contains two sheets with an identical structure. One contains the data about females and the other contains data about males:

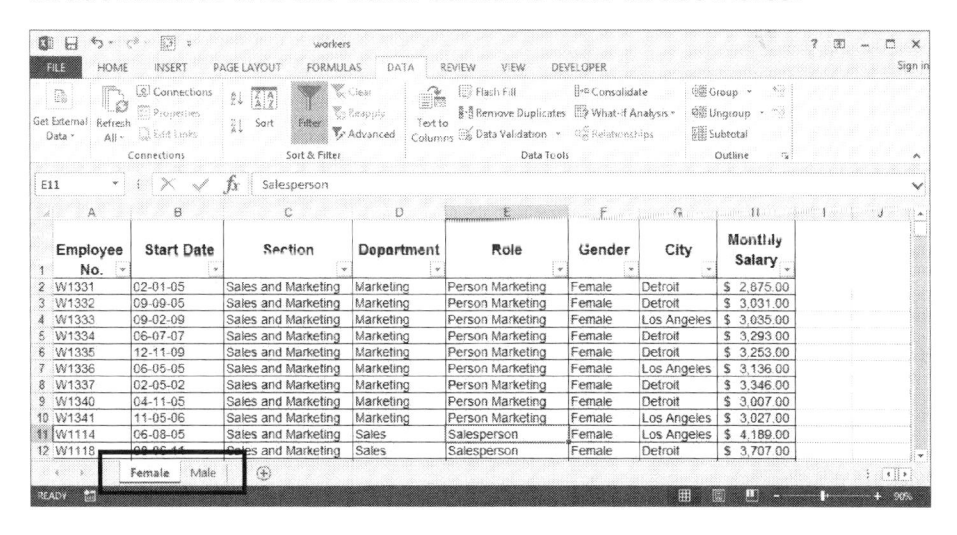

1. On the Quick Access Toolbar, click on the Pivot Tables Wizard (to add a Pivot Table Wizard, see page 144).

2. The following window will appear:

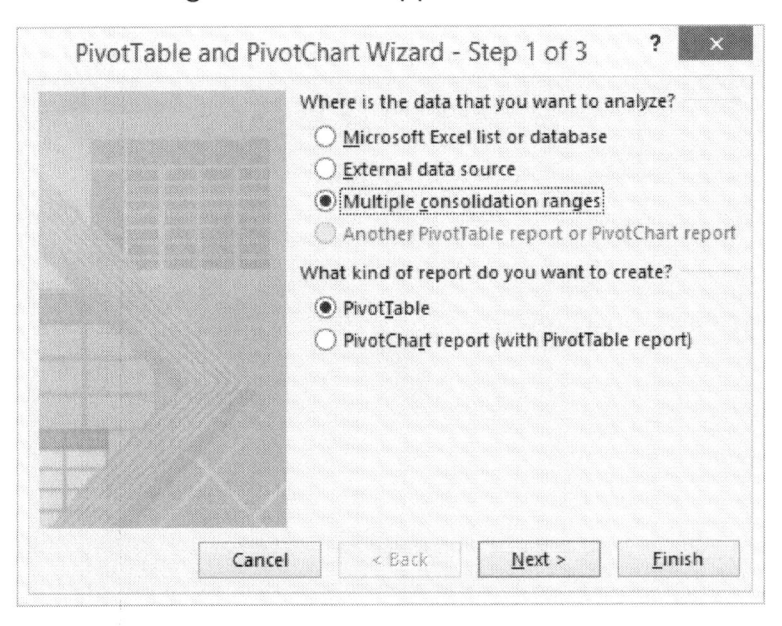

3. Select "**Multiple Consolidation Ranges**".

4. Click `Next >`

5. Select "**Create a single page field for me**":

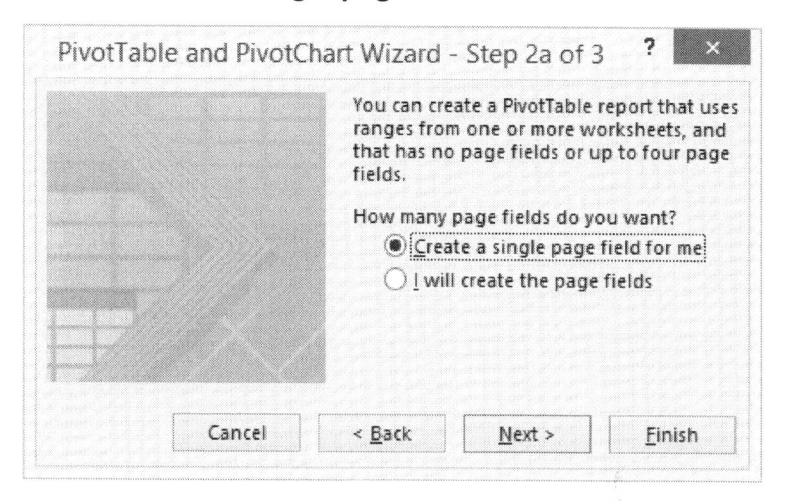

6. Click [Next >]

7. The following window appear:

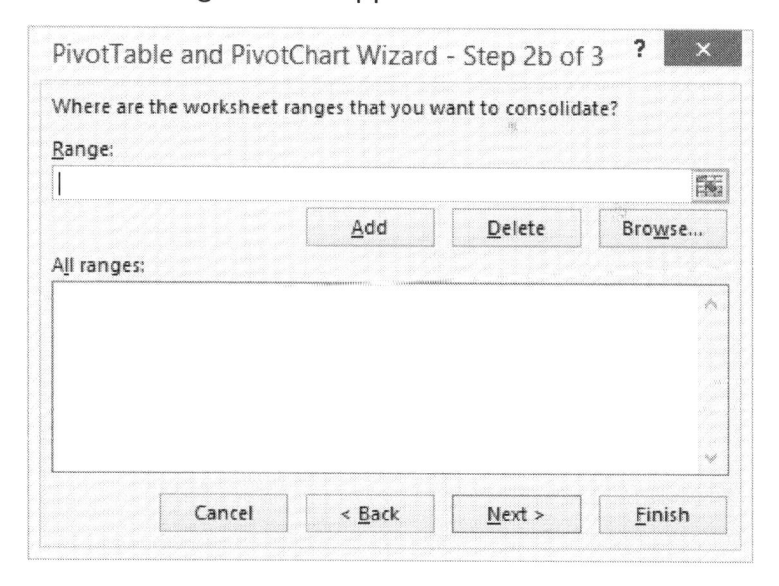

8. Select the desired range in the first worksheet and click [Add]

9. Repeat the operation for each one of the ranges:

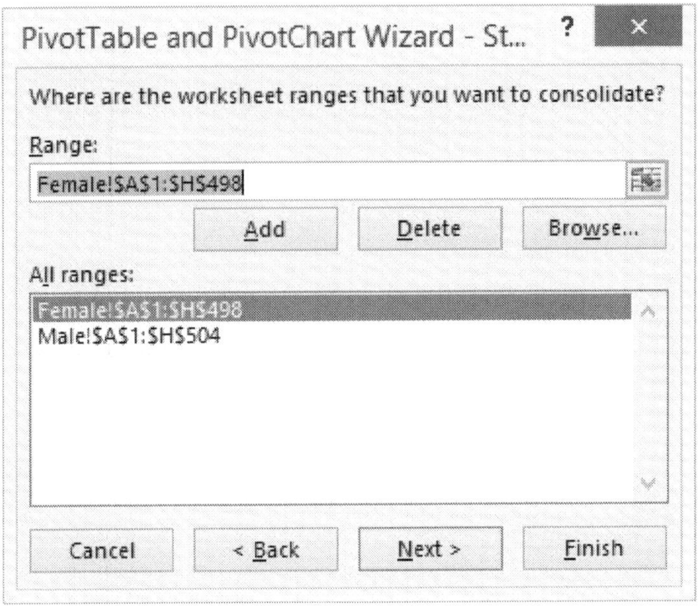
PivotTable and PivotChart Wizard - St...
Where are the worksheet ranges that you want to consolidate?
Range:
Female!$A$1:$H$498
Add
Delete
Browse...
All ranges:
Female!$A$1:$H$498
Male!$A$1:$H$504
Cancel
< Back
Next >
Finish

10. Click 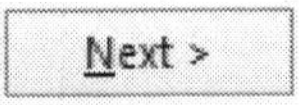
Next >

11. Select the desired location for the pivot table:

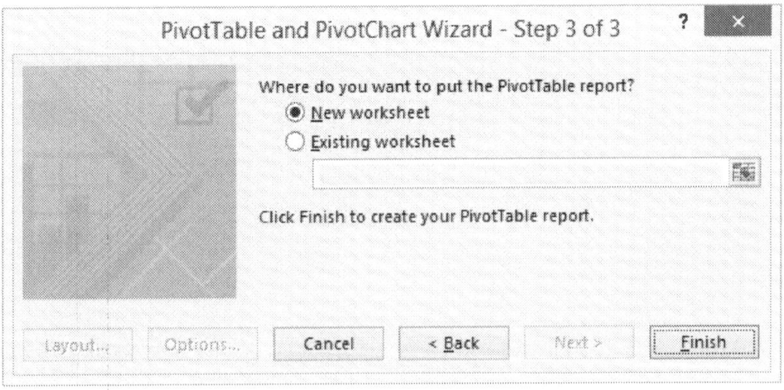
PivotTable and PivotChart Wizard - Step 3 of 3
Where do you want to put the PivotTable report?
New worksheet
Existing worksheet
Click Finish to create your PivotTable report.
Layout...
Options...
Cancel
< Back
Next >
Finish

12. Click 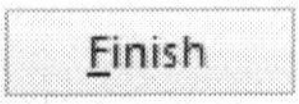
Finish

13. A new pivot table that contains the data from both tables will be created.

14. Please note that the pivot table created will be very limited compared to a pivot table that was created from a single table.

The Data Model

So far, we have dealt with creating pivot tables based on a single data table.

When we wanted to create a pivot table from multiple tables, we had to merge them into one table, usually using the VLOOKUP function.

Excel 2013 introduces, for the first time, the use of the 'Data Model', a term that came from the field of business intelligence (BI) and allows us to create pivot tables from more than one table.

Since we are talking about multiple tables and the relationships between them, the first part of this chapter will be dedicated to a brief acquaintance with some important terms regarding databases.

In the second part of the chapter, we will learn how to create a pivot table that is based upon multiple tables.

Basic terms in databases

Relationships

In order to understand what relationships are, we will use the "Employees" database. However, this time the data comes from two different tables (as opposed to the former chapters, when the data came from a single table):

1. **Employees table** - a table that contains the data of the employees and the department to which they belong:

Emp No.	Dep	Role
W1000	Headquarters	Department Manager
W1001	Headquarters	Department Manager
W1002	Headquarters	Department Manager
W1003	Welding	Manager
W1004	Engraving	Manager
W1005	Sales	Manager
W1006	Marketing	Manager
W1007	Accounting depa	Manager
W1008	Human Resourc	Manager
W1009	Welding	Engineer
W1010	Welding	Engineer
W1011	Welding	Engineer
W1012	Welding	Engineer
W1013	Welding	Engineer

2. **Departments and Sections table** - this serves as an auxiliary table, and specifies to which department each

section belongs:

Dep	Section
Marketing	Sales and Marketing
Sales	Sales and Marketing
Engraving	Manufacturing
Welding	Manufacturing
headquarters	Management
accounting department	Management
Human Resources	Management
Accounting	Management

If we wanted to create a pivot table in Excel 2010 which will show the total salaries in each section, we would have to import the section column from the auxiliary table to our Primary Data Table using VLOOKUP, and only then create a pivot table based on the combined table.

Excel 2013 displays a significant improvement, which is based on the concept of linking two tables, using a common field.

It uses a logical relation between two tables and enables us to take data from one table and, through the common field, associate it with corresponding relevant data from another table.

If you are familiar with the VLOOKUP function, it will be much easier for you to understand, because this function locates corresponding details from one table through the common field, and delivers them to the relevant records in another table.

In our case, the common field is the department field that links the two tables.

Note: the employees table contains the data of 1,000 employees, but the table of departments and sections contains a short list of 7 records only, as that is the number of departments.

If we used the VLOOKUP function to create one table, there would be 1000 additional functions to the data table (a function for each row in the table).

When we logically connect tables, we save the memory from being occupied by this large number of formulas.

Types of Relationship

In general, there are three main types of relationship between tables:

1. **One-to-one** - a 'one-to-one' relationship means that one field of the first table links to only one record in the second table. Similarly one field from the second

table links to only one record in the first table. An example of such a relationship is a data table split into two different tables - the employees table that contains employees' ID and their department, and the salaries table that contains employees' ID and their salaries.

The relationship between these two tables is a one-to-one relationship, since they both contain the same list of employees, and each employee appears only once in each of them.

The division into two tables is done for reasons that are unrelated to the essence of working with databases and can be, for example, security concerns (while the department name of the employee can be visible, their pay data is confidential, and they should not be kept in a table that is visible to everyone), or for the ease-of-use in huge tables with many fields.

2. **One-to-many relationship** - this is when one item in a field in table A can be related to numerous records in table B, whereas one field in table B can be related to only one record in table A.

A good example of this could be the relationship between the employees table and a table documenting the employees' vacations. The employees table contains relevant information about the employees and each of them appears there only once. However, employees can appear in the vacation table many times, according to the number of vacations each of them took.

The relationship between the tables is a one-to-many, since for any employee data in the employees table, there can be multiple records in the vacations table (each employee can go on vacation several times), but for any employee data in the vacations table, there can be only one related record in the employees table, because every employee is documented there only once.

In fact, this is the most common type of relationship.

3. **Many-to-many relationship** - a relationship in which for each record in one table, there can be multiple corresponding records in the second table, and for each record in the second table, there can be many

corresponding records in the first table. The best example of this is students and courses - each student can learn a large number of courses, and on each course there are a large number of students. A relationship of this type is created through two one-to-many relationships.

The possible types of relationships between the data model are one-to-one and one-to-many relationships.

Primary key

A primary key is an identifier of a record. It appears only once in the table, and the record can be identified by it.

Common primary keys are ID, employee number, license number, catalog number, and so on.

The primary key in the employees table is the employee number, but primary keys can also be textual, as in the departments table, where the primary key is the name of the department.

Foreign key

A foreign key is a primary key of one table, which appears in another table.

In contrast to the primary key, which can appear only once in the table, a foreign key can appear in the table more than once. In our case, a department field that is the primary key in the department table, and thus appears only once, serves as a foreign key in the employees table, and appears multiple times.

The following illustration will help you understand:

Every department appears only once in the departments table:

Dep	Section
Marketing	Sales and Marketing
Sales	Sales and Marketing
Engraving	Manufacturing
Welding	Manufacturing
headquarters	Management
accounting department	Management
Human Resources	Management
Accounting	Management

Whereas the departments appear multiple times in the

employees table:

Emp No.	Dep	Role
W1331	Marketing	Person Marketing
W1332	Marketing	Person Marketing
W1333	Marketing	Person Marketing
W1334	Marketing	Person Marketing
W1335	Marketing	Person Marketing
W1336	Marketing	Person Marketing
W1337	Marketing	Person Marketing
W1338	Marketing	Person Marketing
W1339	Marketing	Person Marketing
W1340	Marketing	Person Marketing
W1341	Marketing	Person Marketing
W1112	Sales	salesperson
W1113	Sales	salesperson
W1114	Sales	salesperson

Therefore, the employees table contains two keys: a primary key, which is the employee number, that appears only once, and a foreign key, which is the department name, that can appear several times in the employees table (but only once in the departments table).

The creation of relationships between tables is done through the common key, which is the primary key in the first table, and the foreign key in the second table. In our case, this is the department field.

Creating a pivot table based on two or more tables

The creation of a pivot table that is based on more than one table is done as follows:

1. Create dynamic tables from all the relevant tables in your workbook (see page 34).

2. Create an empty pivot table from one of the tables, by using the Data Model.

3. Create the relationships.

4. Drag the fields to the desired pivot table areas.

Creating the pivot table

After we have connected the two tables, we can create a pivot table that is based on both.

In the first stage, we have to turn the data into a dynamic table, as we learned on page 34 (it is preferable to provide the tables with meaningful names).

Now we can select the employees table and click **INSERT → PivotTable**.

The big change in the Excel 2013 version is the option to add the table to the data model. For this purpose, we check the **"Add this data to the Data Model**" checkbox, as shown in the following window:

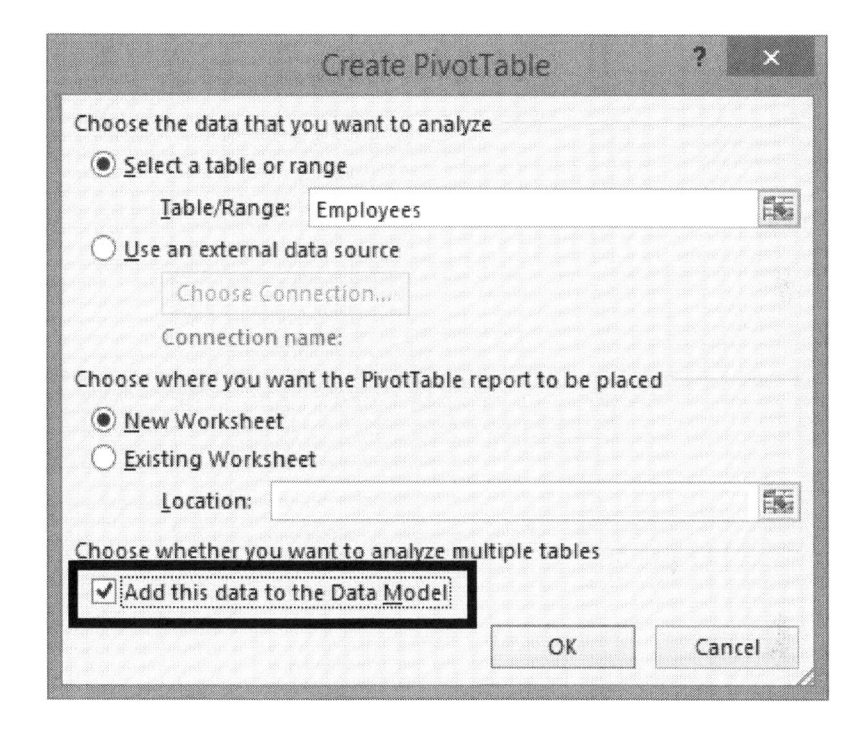

A pivot table will be created, which at first glance seems like a regular pivot table.

Taking a closer look, we can see that two tabs appear under the pivot table fields: "**Active**" and "**All**".

In the "Active" tab, we can see the table that was the source of our pivot table, as can be seen in the following image:

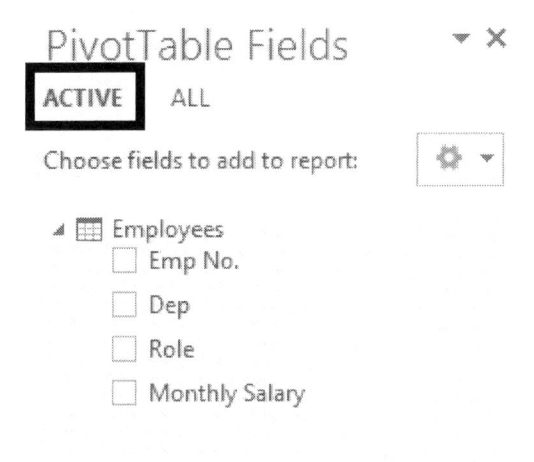

PivotTable Fields

ACTIVE ALL

Choose fields to add to report:

▲ ☐ Employees
    ☐ Emp No.
    ☐ Dep
    ☐ Role
    ☐ Monthly Salary

In the "All" tab we can see that Excel has automatically created a list of all the dynamic tables that are in our workbook.

PivotTable Fields

ACTIVE **ALL**

Choose fields to add to report:

▷ ☐ Departments
▷ ☐ Employees

Clicking on the triangle arrow next to the name of the table will expand it to display the table fields:

PivotTable Fields　▼ ✕

ACTIVE　ALL

Choose fields to add to report:

▲ ▦ Departments
　　☐ Dep
　　☐ Section

▲ ▦ Employees
　　☐ Emp No.
　　☐ Dep
　　☐ Role
　　☐ Monthly Salary

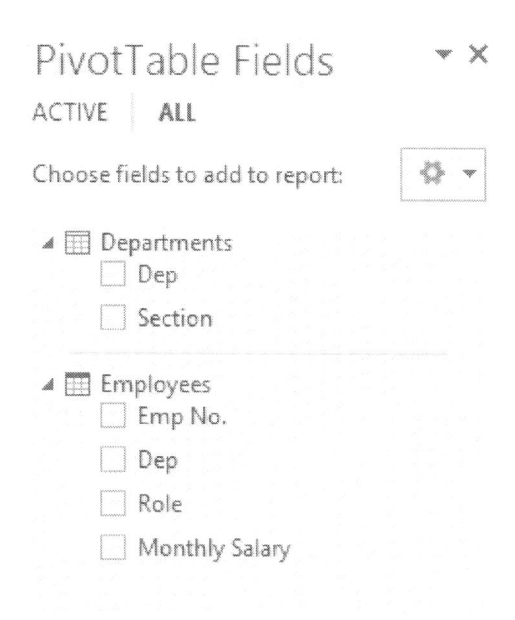

Creating Relationships

Before dragging the fields to the respective areas, we have to create a relationship between the two tables:

Forming a relationship (One to Many):

After we have identified the keys, we need to connect the two tables by forming relations from the foreign key to the primary key (in other words, from the "Many" side to the "One" side). In our case, from the departments column in the employees table to the departments column in the departments table.

Emp No.	Dep	Role	Monthly Salary		Dep	Section
W1331	Marketing	Person Marketing	$2,875.00		Marketing	Sales and Marketing
W1332	Marketing	Person Marketing	$3,091.00		Sales	Sales and Marketing
W1333	Marketing	Person Marketing	$3,035.00		Engraving	Manufacturing
W1334	Marketing	Person Marketing	$3,293.00		Welding	Manufacturing
W1335	Marketing	Person Marketing	$3,253.00		headquarters	Management
W1336	Marketing	Person Marketing	$3,136.00		headquarters	Manufacturing
W1337	Marketing	Person Marketing	$3,346.00		headquarters	Sales and Marketing
W1338	Marketing	Person Marketing	$2,864.00		accounting department	Management
W1339	Marketing	Person Marketing	$3,178.00		Human Resources	Management
W1340	Marketing	Person Marketing	$3,007.00		Accounting	Management
W1341	Marketing	Person Marketing	$3,027.00			
W1112	Sales	salesperson	$3,741.00			
W1113	Sales	salesperson	$4,015.00			
W1114	Sales	salesperson	$4,189.00			
W1115	Sales	salesperson	$3,651.00			
W1116	Sales	salesperson	$3,906.00			
W1117	Sales	salesperson	$3,785.00			
W1118	Sales	salesperson	$3,707.00			
W1119	Sales	salesperson	$3,916.00			
W1120	Sales	salesperson	$4,085.00			
W1121	Sales	salesperson	$4,250.00			

Forming a relationship (One to One):

If our data tables are based on a one to one relationship, for example, a table that contains the employees' numbers and their salaries:

Employee No.	Monthly Salary
W1000	$ 4,602.00
W1001	$ 4,449.00
W1002	$ 5,140.00
W1003	$ 3,990.00
W1004	$ 3,850.00
W1005	$ 4,108.00
W1006	$ 4,304.00
W1007	$ 3,820.00
W1008	$ 3,908.00
W1009	$ 8,113.00
W1010	$ 6,740.00

And a table that contains other details about the employees:

Employee No.	Start Date	Section	Department	Role	Gender	City	Monthly Salary
W1000	12/06/07	Manufacturing	Headquarters	Department Manager	Male	New Jersey	$ 4,602.00
W1001	11/05/07	Sales and Marketing	Headquarters	Department Manager	Female	New Jersey	$ 4,449.00
W1002	05/10/08	Management	Headquarters	Department Manager	Female	Miami	$ 5,140.00
W1003	08/10/09	Manufacturing	Welding	Manager	Male	Miami	$ 3,990.00
W1004	03/04/04	Manufacturing	Engraving	Manager	Male	New Jersey	$ 3,850.00
W1005	08/12/01	Sales and Marketing	Sales	Manager	Male	Miami	$ 4,108.00
W1006	09/08/08	Sales and Marketing	Marketing	Manager	Male	Miami	$ 4,304.00
W1007	12/06/01	Management	Accounting dep	Manager	Female	Detroit	$ 3,820.00
W1008	11/12/04	Management	Human Resourc	Manager	Male	Miami	$ 3,908.00
W1009	09/07/10	Manufacturing	Welding	Engineer	Male	San Diego	$ 8,113.00
W1010	01/11/09	Manufacturing	Welding	Engineer	Male	New Jersey	$ 6,740.00

The creation of a relationship will be from the key in the table that contains the items that should be calculated (in our case – the salary), to the key in the second table.

Creating the Relationship

1. Click on the "**PIVOTTABLE TOOLS**" tab.
2. Select the "**ANALYZE**" tab.
3. Click on "**Relationships**":

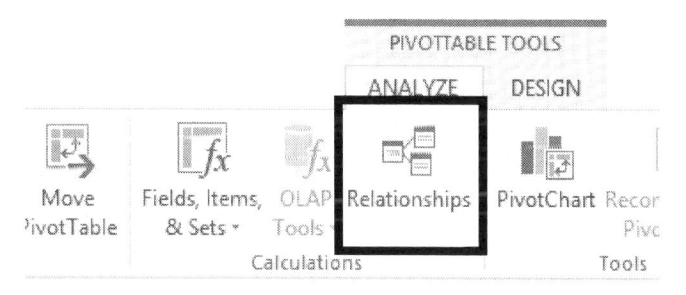

167

4. The following window will open:

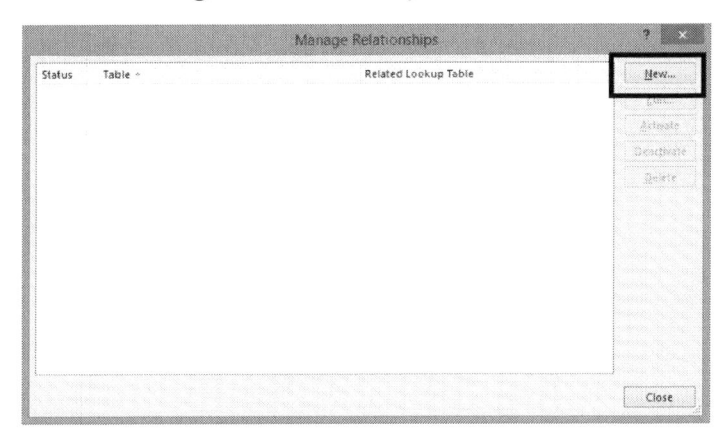

5. Click on New...

6. The relationship window will open:

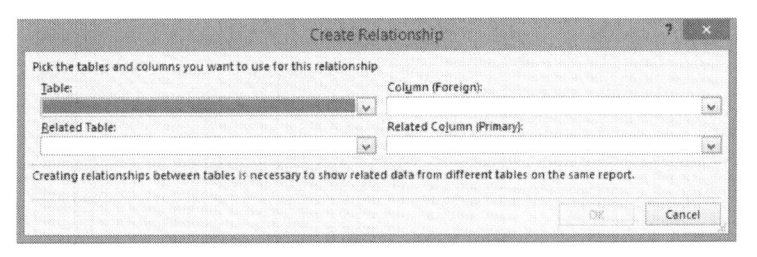

7. The window is divided into two parts:

    - In a "One to Many" relationship the upper part refers to the table that contains the foreign key, and the lower part relates to the table that contains the primary key.

    - In a "One to One" relationship the upper part refers to the table that contains the fields to be calculated and the lower part refers to the other table.

8. Since we have a "One to Many" relationship, we select the employees table and the department column (that serves as the foreign key) in the upper part, whereas in the lower part we select the departments table and the department column (which serves as a primary key in this table):

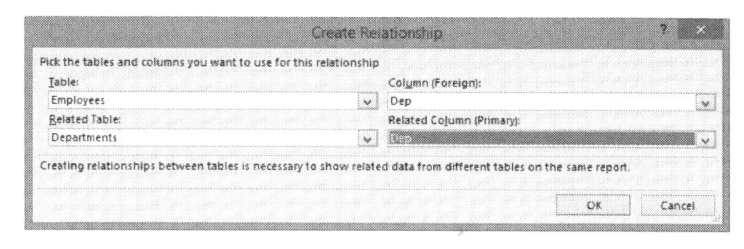

9. Click **OK**

Dragging the fields

After creating the relationships between the 2 tables, we can start dragging the fields to the pivot table.

In our case, we will drag the section out of the departments table to the ROWS and the salaries out of the employees table to the VALUES:

	A	B
3	Section	Sum of Monthly Salary
4	Management	69045
5	Manufacturing	1581664
6	Sales and Marketing	854170
7	Grand Total	2504879

PivotTable Fields

Choose fields to add to report:

- ▲ Departments
  - ☑ **Section**
  - ☐ Department
- ▲ Employees
  - ☐ Employee No.
  - ☐ Start Date
  - ☐ Department
  - ☐ Role
  - ☐ Gender
  - ☐ City
  - ☑ **Monthly Salary**

ROWS: Section
VALUES: Sum of Mont...

We will get the sum of all monthly salaries in each section, even though the data is from two different tables!

And what if we didn't create the relationships in advance?

In the following example we dragged the fields without creating the relations before, and we can see two things:

1. The total payroll in every section is the same (this is actually the sum of the total payroll, without dividing into sections):

Row Labels	Sum of Monthly Salary
Management	2504879
Manufacturing	2504879
Sales and Marketing	2504879
Grand Total	2504879

2. A yellow message bar prompts us to create relationships:

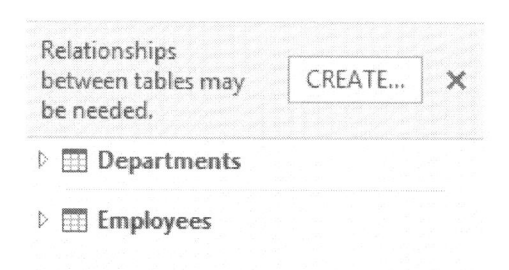

> Relationships between tables may be needed. [CREATE...] ✕
> ▷ ▦ Departments
> ▷ ▦ Employees

Clicking on CREATE... will open the relationship window, and their creation will fix the values in the table.

Distinct Count Functions

In addition to the regular calculations (sum, average, etc.), using the data model allows us to use the new function, "Distinct Count", to count distinct values.

Let's look at the following example:

Suppose we want to know how many different (distinct) roles exist in each section.

1. Drag the section to the rows.

2. Drag the role to the values.

3. The pivot table that was created displays the number of roles in each section, which, for now, is equal to the number of employees in each section:

Row Labels	Count of Role
Management	21
Manufacturing	763
Sales and Marketing	216
Grand Total	1000

4. However, in order to know how many distinct roles exist in each section, we have to right-click on the values field and select "**Summarize values by**" →

"More options":

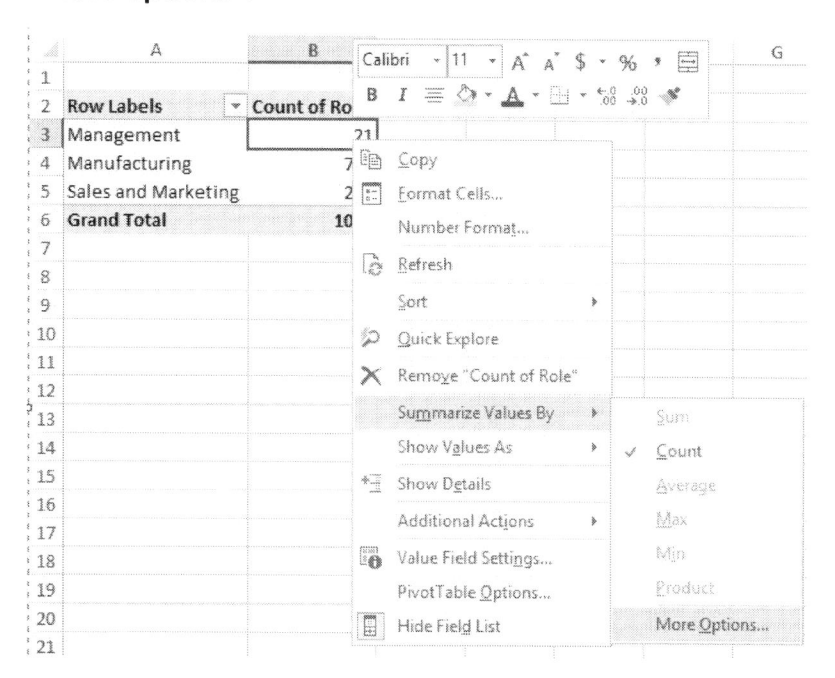

5. Select "Distinct Count":

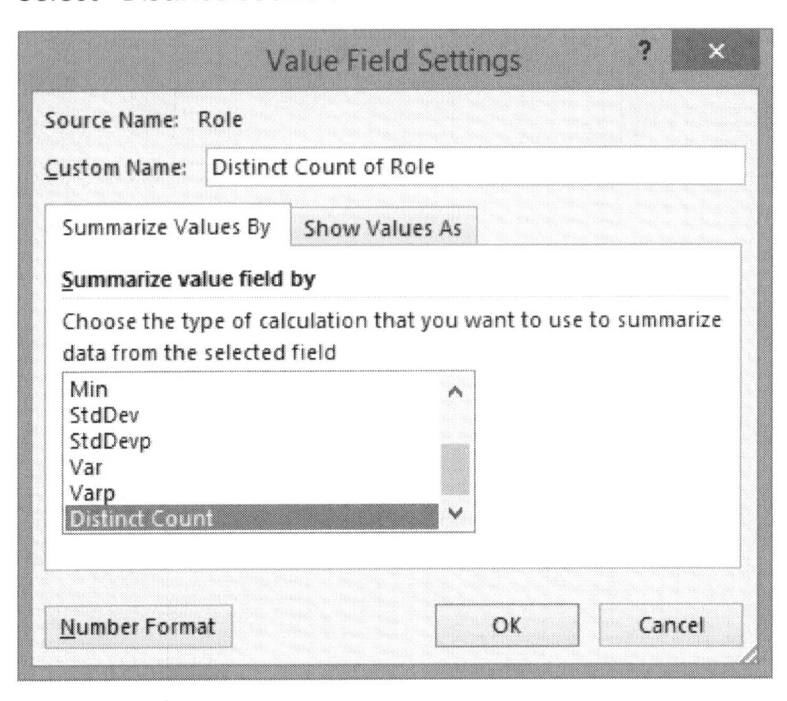

   ## Value Field Settings

   Source Name: Role

   Custom Name: Distinct Count of Role

   Summarize Values By | Show Values As

   Summarize value field by

   Choose the type of calculation that you want to use to summarize data from the selected field

   - Min
   - StdDev
   - StdDevp
   - Var
   - Varp
   - **Distinct Count**

   Number Format | OK | Cancel

6. Click OK

7. A pivot table that shows the number of professions in each section was created:

Row Labels	Distinct Count of Role
Management	6
Manufacturing	4
Sales and Marketing	3
Grand Total	11

8. We can see that there are 6 different roles in management, 4 in manufacturing and 3 different roles in sales and marketing.

The data model limitations

So far, we have seen the significant advantages of working with the data model, but there are also some disadvantages that we have to pay attention to:

Grouping

The first disadvantage is that items that are based on the Data Model cannot be grouped directly.

The way to group them is to add the grouping fields to the data table. That is, if we want to group by months and years, we will add a column to the source table and, using the Month and Year functions, pull out the month and year from the date field. Now we can add these fields to the pivot table to create the desired grouping.

Calculated fields and calculated items

Calculated fields or calculated items cannot be created if the pivot table is based upon the data model (you can do it using the PowerPivot add-in, which is not in the scope of this book).

Refresh

If we have pivot tables that are based on the data model (as we have learned to create in this chapter), and pivot tables based on the cache memory (as we have learned to create in previous chapters), we won't be able to refresh them together by using the "Refresh all" button, and we will have to access each one separately and refresh it.

Displaying the data source (Drill Down)

Double-clicking on a value in the VALUES field returns only a list of the first 1000 records from the source table, and not all the data.

Epilogue

Dear Readers,

Great efforts were made writing this book, in order to convey to you the knowledge we have gained.

However, if there are issues not explained here in the book, and which are of great importance to you, please let us know by email, so we can make even more effort to integrate them into the next edition.

Thank You.

Maayan Poleg and Sahron Barak

Maayan Poleg: info@excel-vba.guru

The book "Excel VBA: for Non-Programmers" (Programming in Everyday Language)

Over the years, Microsoft Excel has become dominant in the field of electronic spreadsheets.

The strength of this software serves the demands of users over the whole world.

However, with the expanding use of the software, some of the end-user requirements are possible only through programming in VBA.

The book "Excel VBA: for Non-Programmers (Programming in Everyday Language)" was written in response to the growing demand for advanced use of the software.

The book was written for:

- Those who want to develop forms for their organization's management

- Those who want to make Microsoft Excel a powerful utility that facilitates their daily work

- The "non-programmers" among us, who have to build those reports in Microsoft Excel over and over again, and want to automate these steps

The book was written by Maayan Poleg, with an understanding of the needs of Microsoft Excel's users, and with the intention "to download the magic" into everyday language.

The author's experience in both VBA programming and training, provided an opportunity to bring this world of development to the inexperienced.

The book is designed for Excel users, who do not have programming backgrounds, but have a desire to make the most of the software. For this reason, the book has been written in an everyday language, reducing the use of technical terms.

You can order the book via Amazon at:
http://amzn.to/1QFp2ic

Made in the USA
Middletown, DE
05 June 2019